Kerry Playwright

John B. Keane. Photograph used by permission of Mercier Press.

Kerry Playwright

Sense of Place
in the Plays of John B. Keane

Sister Marie Hubert Kealy

SUP

Selinsgrove: Susquehanna University Press
London and Toronto: Associated University Presses

Associated University Presses
440 Forsgate Drive
Cranbury, NJ 08512

Associated University Presses
25 Sicilian Avenue
London WC1A 2QH, England

Associated University Presses
P.O. Box 338, Port Credit
Mississauga, Ontario
Canada L5G 4L8

The paper used in this publication meets the requirements of the American National Standard for Permanence of Paper for Printed Library Materials Z39.48-1984.

Library of Congress Cataloging-in-Publication Data

Kealy, Marie Hubert, 1935–
    Kerry playwright : sense of place in the plays of John B. Keane / Marie Hubert Kealy.
      p. cm.
      Includes bibliographical references (p.) and index.
    ISBN 0-945636-54-7 (alk. paper)
      1. Keane, John B., 1928– —Knowledge—Ireland—Kerry. 2. Keane, John B., 1928– —Dramatic works. 3. Kerry (Ireland) in literature. I. Title.
PR6061.E2Z74   1993
822'.914—dc20
                                        92-51001
                                          CIP

PRINTED IN THE UNITED STATES OF AMERICA

Contents

Abbreviations

For ease of reference, all quotations from the plays and other published works of John B. Keane are followed by the appropriate citation. Reference to unpublished material, mainly interviews, are by means of superscript numbers. The following abbreviations, indicating the editions consulted, will be used throughout this text.

BM   *Big Maggie*. Cork: The Mercier Press, 1959.

Bodhran   *The Bodhran Makers*. Dingle: Brandon Book Publishers Ltd., 1986.

Buds   *The Buds of Ballybunion*. Cork: The Mercier Press, 1979.

C   *The Chastitute*. Cork: The Mercier Press, 1981.

Change   *The Change in Mame Fadden*. Cork: The Mercier Press, 1973.

CW   *The Crazy Wall*. Cork: The Mercier Press, 1974.

F   *The Field*. Cork: The Mercier Press, 1965.

Good   *The Good Thing*. Newark, Del.: Proscenium Press, 1978.

H   *Hut 42*. Dixon, Calif.: Proscenium Press, 1962.

HH   *The Highest House on the Mountain*. Dublin: Progress House, 1961.

Hiker   *The Year of the Hiker*. Cork: The Mercier Press, 1963.

M   *Moll*. Cork: The Mercier Press, 1971.

Man   *The Man from Clare*. Cork: The Mercier Press, 1965.

Many   *Many Young Men of Twenty*. Dublin: Progress House, 1961.

Rain   *The Rain at the End of Summer*. Dublin: Progress House, 1967.

S   *Sive*. Dublin: Progress House, 1959.

SG   *Sharon's Grave*. Dublin: Progress House, 1960.

SP   *Self Portrait*. Cork: The Mercier Press, 1954.

Three   *Three Plays: Sive, The Field, Big Maggie*. Rev. ed. Edited by Ben Barnes. Cork: The Mercier Press, 1990.

Acknowledgments

I wish to record my gratitude to the many persons who encouraged me in my writing. My first debt of thanks belongs to my family who inspired and nourished my love of literature, theater, and our Irish heritage.

This study began as a dissertation in the Department of English at the University of Pennsylvania. I am grateful to Cary Mazer, Vicki Mahaffey, and Gerald Weales for their advice and their patient reading of several drafts of the original. I wish to acknowledge the support of my religious community, the Sisters, Servants of the Immaculate Heart of Mary, especially Mother Marie Genevieve to whom I am indebted for the educational opportunities culminating in this text.

Many people assisted me in this work, but I should like to acknowledge the following in particular: John B. Keane and his family for their warm hospitality and their generous encouragement of my research; Ben Barnes, Barry Cassin, and James N. Healy for sharing their experiences in producing Keane's plays; Micheal O'hAodha, Abbey Theatre; Dr. Christopher Murray, University College Dublin; Gus Smith, freelance writer, Dublin; the staff of the National Library, Dublin; Mary Clarke, archivist, Irish Theatre Archives, Dublin; Barbara Durack and Noel Shields of Radio Telefis Eireann; the staff of the University of Pennsylvania Library, particularly the members of the Inter-Library Loan Department; and the Daughters of Charity, Blackrock, for their friendship and hospitality during my visits to Ireland. I wish also to thank The Mercier Press, Cork, Ireland and Progress House, Dublin, Ireland for permission to cite passages from Keane plays published by their houses.

Portions of this study have appeared in different form in the *Irish University Review* and *Notes on Modern Irish Literature*.

Finally, I am indebted to Sister Loretta Maria and Patricia Mehok of Immaculata College for their assistance in preparing and proofreading the manuscript.

Kerry Playwright

Introduction

Contemporary Irish playwrights face the threefold challenge of popular taste, professional critics, and the Irish dramatic tradition. Both audiences and critics receive a new play within the frame of reference established by the great dramatists of the past. Such a reception situates the modern playwright within the history of the Irish theater and also exemplifies the Irishman's devotion to the past which can cripple the creative urge. Consequently, the tensions between modernity and an historic ideal are central to the themes employed by Irish dramatists today. Writers recognize that worldwide acceptance demands that they explore contemporary and universal problems. At the same time, they realize that success depends upon their writing about the world they know. Irish writers risk being termed regional when their reliance upon local sites and characters creates a place somewhat apart from the current milieu. Yet, playwrights like John B. Keane are regional in the best sense because they draw on the importance of place in Irish culture as a way of ordering their perceptions of contemporary society.

Dramatists today, as in the past, project stage images of the Irishman. Whether these figures resemble earlier stereotypes or approach a true definition of Irishness is often difficult to determine; however, stage devices establish the "spirit of place" in each play and give subtle themes a concrete form.

Much of modern Irish drama remains a local phenomenon, but not because of a lack of talent. Robert Hogan notes in his introduction to *Seven Irish Plays* that "the new drama of Ireland is as rich as drama written anywhere else in the world. The reason so little has been heard of it is more a matter of theatrical economics than of dramatic merit."[1] Producers are reluctant to take a chance on regional themes and unknown names in these days when the expenses of mounting a production must be met by the box office returns. Nevertheless, there are prominent tal-

13

ents in the Irish theater, and one of the most significant is John
B. Keane.

Keane's career began in the Amateur Theatre Movement when
the Listowel Drama Group produced his first play *Sive* in 1959.
This play, although rejected by the Abbey Theatre, became an
outstanding success in the regional and All Ireland drama competitions, and it remains one of the most popular plays in Ireland
today. It is a play true to the rural experience and to the rhythms
of the Kerry language. The early rejection of *Sive* by the theater
establishment, in spite of its being similar in style and theme to
the "Abbey plays," suggests that Keane's rural drama departs in
some way from the peasant formula and, thus, deserves critical
attention. Robert Hogan, in the introduction cited above, remarks
that in the newer Irish drama one can find the themes of the
older plays "translated into terms of individual anguish rather
than seen as uniquely national problems."[2] It is the shift from a
national focus to the problems of individuals in rural Ireland
that sets up the possibilities of social commentary within the
tradition of the peasant play.

John B. Keane's plays are representative of the current struggle
between the received traditions and the inroads of the modern
world. His appreciation of place and his adapting the spirit of
his own locale to the stage provides a way into the meaning of
contemporary Irish drama.

A study of the importance of John B. Keane to modern Irish
literature cuts across the genres of drama, fiction, and nonfiction.
A prolific writer in a variety of media, he is best known as a
playwright; however, some contend that Keane is a personality
whose outspoken views on Irish life and mores make him as
much a "character" as any of the personae he has invented.

Keane is certainly a significant feature in the Irish landscape.
He is, as Gus Smith remarked to this author, "a legend in his
own lifetime."[3] He is, more importantly, the voice of the small
town, rural Irish in a country that is becoming urban and cosmo-
politan. At the same time, Keane both criticizes Irish stereotypes
in earlier literature and folk memory and also laments the vanishing social order that is being replaced by television.

This study examines "place" as a way to meaning. It interprets
the use of specific stage conventions as signals of the cultural
heritage of Ireland. Because many of John B. Keane's plays rely

on rural characters and themes, his work aptly illustrates the significance of spirit of place in Irish drama. Regional characters, dialects, songs, and costumes, as well as the cottage setting, provide a frame for the playwright's view of Ireland, and Keane tends toward a critical examination of Irish life within the context of folklore and traditional values.

Place functions as a formal and thematic element in Keane's dramas. Authentic characters, music, and language provide details that evoke the North Kerry landscape; these same conventions comprise a frame of reference for the thematic concerns of his plots. Traditional characters juxtaposed with contemporary issues result in the dual thrust of nostalgia and criticism that marks his plays. Place makes situations specific and local while leading the audience to more general meanings by triggering a variety of associations.

This use of place is the key to John B. Keane's success as a playwright. Brian Cleeve notes that Keane's work "belongs to his countryside as the rocks do. And yet in spite of that, or perhaps because of it, it could be understood by anyone who knows and loves any countryside, even if it was on the other side of the world."[4] Keane's portrayal of regional scenes and characters depends for its effect on their being recognized by the audience. Both the local characteristics and the universality of human types and motives can be found in the Kerry characters that appear in his plays. The conventions of characterization and dialect render his plays concrete and regional. Keane's use of the land and emigration themes links him to the Abbey tradition even while his social criticism breaks with that tradition.

Keane's rural plays are closest to his own experience, and, therefore, more successful than his attempts at the urban problem play. Because the Kerry plays draw on recognition and nostalgia, while often criticizing the traditions that arouse those sentiments, they are Keane's dramatic strength. This study, therefore, will focus on some of the plays set in Kerry. Other critical approaches might focus on plays like The Good Thing and The Change in Mame Fadden; these plays offer astute observations on human life and relationships. They have, however, been less successful than the rural plays and less obviously rely on a sense of place for their meaning.

This exploration of Keane's plays begins with an overview of his literary career to date and a definition of "place" as a tool for dramatic criticism. The remaining chapters examine Keane's folk plays and his use of specific stage conventions to evoke the Kerry countryside. The study concludes by discussing the traditional themes of land, emigration, and marriage as vehicles for social criticism in his later plays. Citations from the plays, in this work, are from the original editions unless the revised version is specified in the text. New acting versions of *Sive*, *The Field*, *Big Maggie*, and *The Year of the Hiker* have appeared since 1985, when Ben Barnes began to take a fresh look at Keane's work. Except for *Big Maggie*, which has a new ending, the two-act versions do not differ significantly from the language and action of the originals. The revisions in *Big Maggie* will be examined as part of the discussion of the play.

The literary landscape of Keane's plays forms a relationship between the artist and his audience based on their shared heritage. An understanding of rootedness and dislocation in contemporary Irish drama may also provide a method for interpreting dramatic conventions and stage space in other plays. It suggests, in the view of this critic, that an individual steeped in the lore of his own region can speak for an entire generation.

Keane's plays are very successful at the box office, but they are more often praised as entertainment than as serious drama. A close study of their impact on the audience, however, reveals a thread of satire which makes Keane an important voice on the Irish theatrical scene. Recognition is the key to his popularity. Keane's deft characterization of well-known types from the Kerry countryside matches the perceptions and memories of his audiences. Both urban and rural audiences respond to the comedic exaggerations of flaws and foibles that recall for them the milieu in which they were reared.

There is a duality in Keane's portrayals: he attacks with laughter the narrowness of the institutions that constrict individuality, yet he expresses a nostalgia for the old days that have disappeared. Such a dual vision is Keane's share of the satiric gift. He presents things as they are and he longs for what they might be. Keane does not offer any formula for achieving the ideal. He, like modern Ireland herself, seems to hover between a celebration of the opportunities of the present and a homesickness for the past.

1

Landscape of a Writer

John B. Keane's personal history shares the shaping influence of place with the history of the Irish theater. Although difficult to define, spirit of place colors and orders one's way of seeing. When it has been embodied in dramatic conventions, the sense of place evokes all the historical and cultural resonances particular to a specific locale. Consequently, folklore, religion, and local customs determine the author's use of stage space, characters, language, and properties. The levels of meaning emerge both through the actors' interpretations and the responses that the recognition of the common "place" generates in the audience. This recognition predisposes the spectators to appreciate the author's observations on contemporary life and his criticism of social institutions.

Much of Keane's literary output owes its inspiration to rural Kerry in which he lives, and his most successful plays draw their strength from the Irish peasant tradition. In fact, place is so central to his work that Keane's gifts of character and dialogue falter when he attempts problem plays in an urban setting. His own place is the West of Ireland with all the cultural and historical nuances associated with that region.

The West is the Gaeltacht, the last surviving bastion of Irish speakers; therefore, the West has been associated with unspoiled "Irishness," as distant in thought and culture from the urban East as from a foreign country. Those who live beyond the Pale have often been considered the true Irish. It was to the West, "to hell or Connaught," that the troops of Cromwell drove the native Irish in order to effect an English settlement, and it was the poorer West that suffered most from the Great Famine of the 1840s and the subsequent evictions. Thus, the imagination of nationalism and rebellion enshrines the West with its peasant population as the true soul of the Irish heritage, and Yeats, the spokesman for the Celtic Revival, sought in the peasantry of the West the appropriate inspiration for a national literature.

This sense of place is the clue to much of Irish writing. To be aware of the cultural landscape is to be in touch with the Irish imagination. Individual authors rarely depict the whole of Ireland in their works, but there is a sense of their being steeped in the places of their personal experience. The trait, described by Sean O'Faolain, of combining a pride in their racial identity with "an equally strong insistence on their regional otherness"[1] may have been politically impractical for the ancient Celts, but it remains the specific contribution of Irish writers. From particular experience they derive the understanding of the human condition that speaks to every audience. The landscape of Ireland is richer in time than in extent, and the unexpected levels of history and magic which startle the visitor are the commonplaces of the native imagination. One cannot encounter the speech of the Irish without entering the world in which the old gods have not entirely surrendered their places to Christianity and the old wars are remembered in story and song. If this richness exists in daily conversation, how much more does it influence the mind and art of the professional writer. It should be no surprise, then, that John B. Keane is, first of all, a Kerryman.

Kerry is an area of varied and breathtaking landscape. The Kingdom, as it is called, is bordered by the counties of Clare, Limerick, and Cork and by the Atlantic Ocean, and its natural beauty attracts hundreds of visitors annually. Ancient and modern life exist side by side in the Kingdom, a condition easily demonstrated by the annual Puck Fair. Held in the West Kerry village of Killorglin, situated on the well-known "Ring of Kerry," the fair continues even today as one of the major festivals of the summer. Although it is an ordinary fair devoted to the sale of livestock, that purpose can be obscured by the pagan rites that dominate the three-day event. A great Puck goat presides over the fair from his throne in the town square, and the pubs never close. The fair is a large boisterous event, an antique pagan remnant in twentieth-century Catholic Ireland. The people of Kerry, too, are larger-than-life because, as John B. Keane himself insists, they reflect the landscape which surrounds them; therefore, the "Texas of Ireland" can boast of invincible football teams and marvelous gifts of language.[2] The Cahills' description of the country confirms Keane's view: "Nowhere else does physiognomy correspond so closely to geography. Kerry people seem to have sprung from Kerry earth—massive, dark, and rough—but from their white-blue eyes, 'cold as the March wind,' shines the same luminosity that is refracted through Kerry air."[3] Kerry is a place apart. It is as far in attitude and spirit from Dublin as it is from America or England. North Kerry, Keane's region, is separate, too, from the Lakes of Killarney and the Dingle Peninsula— the Kerry that the tourists frequent. It is an agricultural area dependent largely on dairy cattle. It is a region in which the Irish love of land is marked by seemingly endless talk of the wetness or dryness of the fields and the quality of the grass.

This is the Kerry in which John B. Keane was born and where he has chosen to remain. In October 1985, during an interview at his home, Keane remarked that there is something in the sounds and atmosphere of one's own region that both invigorates and inspires an individual. "I was lucky . . . I was born in a town which is surrounded by a river." A river, he explained, exerts a sort of discipline; it teaches the rhythms of life: "It has its dry time, but it is still, nevertheless, a river with a vast repertory of beautiful tunes." The land and the river come to life in the characters of North Kerry who people John B. Keane's plays, and the larger-than-life figures depict the virtues and faults of his own area.

John Brendan Keane, born at 45 Church Street in Listowel, County Kerry on 21 July 1928, is the son of William B. Keane and Hannah Purtill Keane, the fourth child in a family of five boys and four girls. He was educated at Listowel Boys' School and St. Michael's College, Listowel, which he completed with an Honors Leaving Certificate in 1946. He was apprenticed to a pharmacist in Listowel for four years until he emigrated to Northampton, where he held a variety of jobs, including two years as a furnace operator at British Timken. His experience made him acutely sensitive to the plight of the Irish emigrant, a theme that recurs in his later writing. Forced to look for employment abroad, Keane, unlike many of his generation, did not permit his time in England to lengthen into permanent separation from his roots. He returned to Listowel, and, for a few years, resumed work as a pharmacist's assistant. Keane and Mary

O'Connor were married on 5 January 1955 in Knocknagoshel Church. They have three sons, William, Conor, and John, one daughter Joanna, and three granddaughters. Shortly after his marriage, Keane purchased a public house at 37 William Street and began the business which has remained part of his career until the present.

Keane has the Irishman's gift for story-telling and of recapturing the full flavor of an incident. He describes his development as a writer in his memoir, *Self-Portrait*, in which he recalls the influence of his father, a teacher in a national school, on his early reading. Both the characters he met in fiction and those he encountered during the summers he spent in the Stacks mountains fed his imagination. Keane notes that the terrain afforded both mystery and beauty, and he recalls that the colorful characters had an aura of magic to a boy from town. He writes:

> Those were wonderful days and it was there, for the first time, that I met characters who mattered and people who left a real impression. These were lively and vital people composed of infinite merriment and a little sadness. They lived according to their means and if you didn't like them you could leave them. (SP 11)

Those characters and the stories told at the fireside have surfaced again and again in Keane's stories and plays, and his instinctive gifts, an ear for dialogue and the capacity to reproduce the idiom of his own region, have contributed greatly to his achievement.

Success, however, did not come easily. Keane had no formal training in writing and has moved from amateur to professional status largely by his own efforts. His beginnings were often disappointing for, although his poems began to appear in local papers shortly after he finished secondary school, Keane did not write seriously until he was living in England. He produced a novel, poems, stories, and essays, but publication eluded him. Finally, in the summer of 1952, he received payment for a piece of writing (SP 58). While this success spurred him to continue writing, Keane's publishing record did not improve until several years after his return to Ireland.

Keane's inspiration to write for the stage came as a result of his seeing the Listowel Drama Group's production of Joseph Tomelty's tragedy *All Soul's Night*. He began his first play *Sive* that very night, and the work was produced by the same company of amateurs on 2 February 1959. The play went on to win at regional competitions and won first place at the All-Ireland Drama Festival held at Athlone in April 1959. This success launched Keane's playwriting career, but professional recognition did not come immediately. In spite of the national honors *Sive* had received, the Abbey Theatre would not consider a production of the play. However, The Southern Theatre Group, a professional company based in Cork and directed by James N. Healy, acquired the rights to *Sive* and produced the play successfully in Cork, Dublin, and other cities. *Sive* has been revived frequently and remains a very popular play. Nineteen plays followed *Sive*, and most of them appeared in the provinces before being produced in Dublin. As a result of his experience, Keane maintains a certain bitterness toward Dublin critics which his friends contend is an understandable reaction of a rural writer. Gus Smith adds that, while the urban-rural tension is always present, the most important thing about John B. Keane is that he did not permit the disappointment over *Sive* to deter him from writing.[4]

The themes of Keane's plays reflect the influence of the amateur theater movement that was prominent in Ireland in the 1950s. It was a movement influenced by the style and standards of the Abbey Theatre; consequently, realistic "kitchen" drama dominated the repertory. Keane followed the Abbey tradition, but wrote more forceful works than were in fashion at the National Theatre at the time. This fact seems to account for the rejection of *Sive* by the company. Remembering that period, Gus Smith comments that there was no excuse for the refusal; *Sive* was an Abbey play. He suggests that there must have been some theater politics at work—someone on the board who could not handle the theme and the violence.[5]

Ironically, as time went on, Keane, more than any other contemporary playwright, carried on the Abbey Theatre's time-honored themes: land, emigration, and the trials of love in a rural environment. Keane's most successful plays from *Sive* (1959) to *The Chastitute* (1981) illustrate both the variety of his interests and the development of his art; they demonstrate also his abiding interest in ordinary people and the frustrations they experience.

The development of Keane's playwriting career occurred at the same time as a revitalization of Irish drama in the 1960s and 1970s and the opening of the country to larger influences through television. The time was ripe for challenging old ideas and authorities, and the younger Irish playwrights took a new position on the traditional themes of marriage, land, religion, and politics. Some playwrights, e.g., Tom Kilroy and Tom Murphy, challenged the status quo by flaunting the sexual taboos and experimenting with form and language as ways of exploring the human personality. In this company, Keane's treatment of land and marriage is conventional; however, his characters, especially the female characters, offer a criticism of Irish society that would have been impossible in the 1940s and 1950s.

Keane's early plays *Sive, Sharon's Grave* (1960), *The Highest House on the Mountain* (1960), and *The Year of the Hiker* (1962) owe much to the folk tradition in Irish theater; at the same time they focus on the genuine problems of rural Ireland in the mid-twentieth century. His use of the folk motifs manages to create a tension between the received tradition of family life and rural society and the struggle for individuality that marks all modern literature. Place, then, is the condition against which the human struggle ensues. Keane's later dramas portray modern life in rural communities and depend on realistic details rather than folk devices for their power of place. Keane's concerns range from land greed and financial security in *The Field* (1965) and *Big Maggie* (1969) to sexual mores and problems of personal fulfillment in *The Chastitute. Many Young Men of Twenty* (1961) and *Hut 42* (1962) draw on Keane's personal experience in England and demonstrate his continuing interest in the conditions that force young people to emigrate from Ireland. His depiction of individual struggles with identity, power, and sexual frustration contributes memorable characters in *The Man from Clare* (1962), *Moll* (1971), *The Change in Mame Fadden* (1971), *The Crazy Wall* (1973), and *The Chastitute* (1981). His best plays draw on the landscape and characters of his native Kerry; when Keane attempts to draw urban characters and settings, his plays are less successful with audiences.

An eloquent example of Keane's dependence on the sense of place is *The Man from Clare*. In this play, the playwright exploits the Irishman's love of sports and the traditional rivalries between the counties in order to express individual pain. Each of the major characters abandons the mask that has been a protection or a symbol of status and exposes his or her deepest emotions honestly. Complicated motives and frustrations appear against the familiar background of a football match. The protagonist, Padraic, realizes that his success at football has kept him from realizing the importance of other aspects of life. His trainer Daigen admits that he has lived vicariously through the fame of his protégée. Morisheen Brick's only concern is to marry his daughter to anyone who will take her; he fails to realize that his insistence has made her even more self-conscious. These men and Morisheen's daughter Nellie are thrust together by a football match between Kerry and Clare. Padraic's prowess fails him in this important game, and his fans and teammates abandon the fallen idol. Against the portrayal of the fickleness of fame, Keane introduces the personal concerns of the major characters. The concrete references to the game set up a familiar scene for the audience; an apparently ordinary football story becomes a means of illustrating the substitutions people make instead of facing themselves. Dan Donovan, director of the original production, writes in the introduction to *The Man from Clare:*

> We see a positive development towards maturity by a character Padraic who through an obsession with sport: partly personal, partly imposed, has only half-lived. But the Man from Clare fights a battle with himself and his environment and emerges belatedly into the full maturity of manhood. (Man 10)

John B. Keane draws his plays from his experience as a resident of a small country town. His window on the street gives him a view of a cosmos in which every type has a particular niche, and there is rarely a locale so class-conscious as a small town. Distinctions of property, occupation, and education mark each resident; one either has been born in the region or one remains a newcomer, even after living there for years. To belong to the land, the region, is a special distinction, and to have to leave, for whatever reason, is a great misfortune. Consequently, the themes of emigration and return are often the focus of Irish dramatic literature, and, particularly, of Keane's plays.

Within the caste system of the rural town one also meets the distinction of name and family; spinsters and bachelors endure another kind of exile unless they have managed to find a way of attaining authority in a household. Keane deals with those who make power their goal and with those who live in spiritual exile.

Such explorations of human isolation work well when they are seen in a rural setting, as in *The Chastitute;* however, when Keane attempts to situate his characters in an urban setting, *The Good Thing* and *The Change in Mame Fadden,* his power fails him. Although Keane's view of the world has shifted somewhat in the course of his career from the folk idiom of his first plays to a more modern stance, his most successful plays are still those set in his native Kerry.

Some of the later plays have touched on subjects that earlier Irish playwrights avoided. James N. Healy attributes to this fact, and not the urban setting, the weaknesses in *The Good Thing* and *The Change in Mame Fadden.* He contends that Keane has capitulated to the taste of the Dublin critics and stifled the very thing that is his forte.[6] Healy's opinion has merit; however, this writer contends that the change in setting is more important than the change of theme. Both plays, although differing in subject, deal with loneliness and spiritual separation from one's family. These motifs also appear in Keane's rural dramas, and plays like *Moll* and *The Chastitute* have enjoyed great success.

Many of Keane's recent plays, both rural and urban, have taken a more ironic, and therefore more modern, view of exploitation. *Big Maggie* and *The Rain at the End of Summer* share this darker vision. They portray self-centered individuals who, despite their best efforts, find themselves rejected by their families. Always, Keane's interest is in people, and, as Eileen Moriarty suggests, "He never ceases to rebel against the web of social injustice, the evils of migration, and the hypocrisy and cruelty of established morality."[7]

Along with his plays, Keane has produced poetry, essays, and fiction. He is well known for his "letter" portraits of well-known Irish characters: the Parish Priest, the T.D., the Matchmaker, the love-hungry farmer, and his essays have the same earthy appeal as his plays. Since his last play *The Chastitute* was produced in 1981, Keane has published *The Man of the Triple Name,* a tribute to a Kerry matchmaker (1984), two collections of essays—*Owl Sandwiches* (1985) and *Love Bites* (1991)—and two novels, *The Bodhran Makers* (1986) and *Durango* (1991).

John B. Keane regularly contributes essays to *The Limerick Leader, The Evening Herald* (Dublin), *The Irish Echo,* and *The Kingdom.* These articles evolve from his observations of small town life and the characters he meets in his public house. Keane is able to distill from his experience insightful and humorous accounts of daily life, and his popularity is an indication of how often his readers identify with his reflections. Both his essays and his very pointed comments on well-known Irish figures, in his Letters, sharply, but kindly, criticize the structures of Irish society that inhibit the personal fulfillment of individuals. Although Keane is familiar to many people as a columnist and as a personality, his concerns and the characters he creates come to life most fully in his major plays and in his fiction.

Of all Keane's nondramatic works, *The Bodhran Makers*, his first novel, is the most significant. It is a major contribution to modern Irish fiction because it not only examines the roots of contemporary social problems in Ireland but also pulls together Keane's lifetime of reflection on certain central themes: poverty, sexual frustration, repressive moral climate, and emigration. In light of this work, Keane's essays, Letter series, and even his plays, have been rehearsals for his well-known characters and clear-eyed, crisp observation of Irish rural life. In the novel, he brings together all the major themes of his plays and portrays also the tensions between past and present in his representation of the town and country figures and in his depiction of ancient folk customs in a contemporary setting.

In the novel, as in his plays, Keane is sympathetic to the ordinary individuals trapped by the religious or social status quo in an unhappy marriage or an unfulfilled single state. He presents as the reason for emigration both the grinding poverty of rural life, with the uncertainties of the harvest, and the repressive moral climate under the control of certain clergy. Keane does not present the Church as having failed the people for he does draw priest characters who are sympathetic, although powerless because of the authority of the Canon. It is the authority structure he deplores, noting that even the Bishop's suggestion of retirement does not move the Parish Priest who is out of touch with the people of his parish. In such a power structure, both the young priests and the parishioners suffer. The good parishioners (wealthy) and the flatterers flourish.

Ultimately, Keane places the blame on those who wield influence in the town; he takes his whip to the merchants and the housekeeper—the economic power and the informer. In *The*

Bodhran Makers, Keane offers a mature statement of all the concerns of his plays and the observations of his essays in one brilliantly conceived novel.

Although Keane's plays enjoy box office success, his work has received mixed reviews from critics and literary historians. Keane dismisses some of these judgments as academic exercises of individuals who are out of touch with real life and points to the success of his plays at the box office.[8]

Since 1985, revivals of Keane's major plays, directed by Ben Barnes, have brought the playwright renewed prominence, and, although Keane resists rewriting, he has permitted Barnes great freedom in producing the plays for contemporary audiences. Barnes has edited the plays and has succeeded, as he describes it, in "mining the gold" from scenes that were overwritten in the originals.[9] The cuts in *Sive* are the most severe, and Keane has written a new ending for *Big Maggie*, although the spirit of the originals remains. The plays continue to explore the social issues with no loss of humor or folk appeal. Barnes hopes that the two-act versions of the plays will become the standard acting versions.[10] In support of this view, the revised texts of *Sive*, *The Field*, and *Big Maggie* have been published by Mercier Press (1990).

Ben Barnes has also prepared a revised edition of *The Year of the Hiker* (1991), and Mick Lalley's portrayal of Hiker Lacey was one of the triumphs of the Dublin season in 1990. Following that success, Groundwork, the company formed in 1987 by Barnes and Arthur Lappin, mounted a production of *Moll* in 1991. Barnes contends that although Keane's total body of work has been diluted by the sheer entertainment values of plays like *Moll* and *The Buds of Ballybunion*, his major plays *The Field* and *Sive* are as great as any of the classics of Irish theater. He places Keane's best work beside Synge's *Playboy of the Western World* and O'Casey's *The Plough and the Stars*. Barnes disputes the argument that plays set in the fifties and sixties depict an Ireland that is no longer relevant to the contemporary theatergoer. He believes that there is something in the Irish psyche that will not change and suggests that the attitude toward land, for example, is embedded in the race memory and will live on.[11] This view accounts for his assessment of Keane's popularity and explains the director's desire to revive all of Keane's plays. It accounts, too, for Barnes's decision to have the child Leamy remain in the pub as a hidden witness to the final scene of *The Field*. The boy, in his decision to remain silent, becomes a symbol of the continuation of the racial memory; the knowledge of Bull's guilt and the struggle between the love of land and the power of the bureaucracy will be perpetuated in the coming generation (Three 167).

Like Barnes, Gus Smith, free-lance writer and former drama critic of *The Sunday Independent*, believes that characters like Maggie and Bull McCabe will remain interesting and important figures in Irish drama, much like O'Casey's Joxer. "In the long run," he notes, "a playwright is judged on the durability of his characters." At the same time, Smith admits that some of Keane's characters and themes are alien to urban life, while others, such as greed for land, will always remain. He suggests that plays like *Sive* will always live because the power comes from within the work and is not affected by changing externals in the social order. Smith agrees that the new editions have contributed to the continued success of the plays. He states that a playwright's work has life beyond the original production and that a good play benefits from a new mind (director) looking at the work. Because Keane often overwrites, Smith recognizes the importance of Ben Barnes's role in recasting the plays in two-act versions more suitable for a contemporary audience.[12] Whatever the source of his hold on the audience, John B. Keane is enjoying a renewed interest in his plays. The seats are filled night after night, and this is the true test of popular theater.

In spite of such enduring popularity, Keane's lack of recognition outside of Ireland continues to puzzle many of his fans, although Jim Sheridan's film adaptation of *The Field*, starring Richard Harris as Bull McCabe, has brought Keane some international attention. One answer may be the financial risk involved in mounting an international tour, and Mary Keane suggests that it is partly his own fault that her husband is not well known in the United States. She cites his frequently repeated remark that a writer's job is to write—not to promote himself.[13] Keane carefully guards his writing time; however, he expressed to this writer the hope that his association with Ben Barnes and the Groundwork Company will lead to productions of his plays in the United States and on the Continent.[14] The future does hold plans for revivals and filmmakers are interested in several plays and *The Bodhran Makers.*

Critics may be divided about his place in literary history, and he may not be well known abroad, but John B. Keane is certainly the most popular of the contemporary Irish playwrights. He has received a variety of awards in recognition of his contributions to Irish literature. Keane is a member of Aosdana, the Irish Academy of Arts, and past president of Irish P.E.N.; he has been awarded honorary degrees by both Trinity College, Dublin, where he has recently placed his manuscripts, and Marymount Manhattan College in New York. Since 1985, the new productions have revived interest in Keane's work and enhanced his popularity in Ireland. He has received *The Sunday Tribune* Award for Literature (1986), *The Sunday Independent* Special Arts Award (1986), and the American-Irish Award for Literature (1988). He was named Kerryman of the Year in 1989 and merited the People of the Year Award in 1990. In 1991, he was awarded honorary life membership in the Royal Dublin Society. For more than twenty years, Keane has been one of the major contributors and organizers of the annual Writers' Week held in Listowel in the spring. He is a vital part of the Irish literary scene.

In all his writing, Keane demonstrates his acute observation of the strengths and weaknesses of human nature. His criticism of the religious, economic, and political systems never proclaims revolution or despair, although his portrayals are often stark beneath the laughter. Keane calls for compassionate understanding of human limitations. His work suggests that the individual's struggle for recognition does not differ appreciably from the position of Ireland today. The nation, in its sense of self, hovers between its Gaelic past and the demands of the modern world. The national identity continues to be a vital question for the Irish writer. John B. Keane, by his exploration of the Kerry countryside, proposes that the question will never be addressed satisfactorily by those who abandon their roots. His plays, though critical of Irish institutions, emphasize Keane's belief that one must be true to oneself and compassionate toward others. In this context, sense of place is a share in the communal heritage of the nation and an extension of one's sense of self.

2

Sense of Place, National Identity, and Irish Drama

Dramatists today, as in the past, project stage images of the Irishman. Whether these figures resemble earlier stereotypes or approach a true definition of Irishness is often difficult to determine. Such devices within each work establish the "spirit of place" and contribute to understanding the themes of the plays.

Stereotypes of the Irish, perpetuated in English popular literature, have resulted both in a sense of cultural inferiority and an attitude of resentment among the Irish. The Celtic Literary Revival sought to counter such images by embodying in the peasant everything that was good about Ireland. Peasant life became the gauge of Irishness, and, ultimately, a cultural and political ideal. Archaic Ireland had a great appeal for Yeats, Synge, and Lady Gregory, and in their reaction against the English stereotypes, they created a type of their own, the peasant—Catholic, republican, and Irish-speaking—who represented the purest ideals of the colonized nation. These ideals were at the same time political and aesthetic. The leaders of the Revival recognized the spiritual depth of the Celtic viewpoint, a stance that further separated Ireland from the commercial and materialistic currents in European civilization. It is not difficult to understand, then, the political thrust of early twentieth-century Irish literature and its insistence on establishing an identity separate from England. The problem of identity, however, encompasses more than national independence and the revival of the Gaelic language and the legendary past. There are attitudes derived from specific locales and physical divisions within Ireland that mold an individual's sense of personal and political identity. A spirit of place, although difficult to define, must be recognized as a shaping influence on the contemporary writer.

Place is actually more vital to a sense of Irishness than language. In the Irish tradition of story-telling, the landscape teems with personal and communal history. Names of mountains and streams recall the ancient gods, and every townland preserves the legends of local heroes. Each site has its own tale, preserved in its Gaelic name, but language is not the essential thing. It is the sense of place, a spiritual bond, that provides a link between details and meaning. The stories are complete only when the listeners share the worldview of the community. Like other cultures isolated from the mainstream by time or distance, Ireland has maintained a folk relationship with the land. Therefore, its literary works often draw their imagery and power from a sense of rootedness and shared traditions. Professor Estyn Evans identifies this elusive quality in his study of Ireland's cultural geography. He describes it as a dynamic relationship between life and the land, past and present, in which both the environment and the inhabitants are agents.[1] His view is reinforced by Sean O'Faolain who remarks that any character study of the Irish must take into account the links with pagan prehistory that remain to this day.[2] Evans would describe these links as cultural landscape.

Irish poetry, in particular, can be distinguished by the richness of its references to specific places and the personification of the country in female figures, originally deities who symbolized the fertility of the land. The Anglo-Irish poets used these figures as political emblems and named them "Cathleen ni Houlihan" and "Dark Rosaleen," but Evans notes that the older literature had a "sense of the harmony and mystery of man's place in nature" and an awareness that the gods were present in the land itself.[3] This pagan communion with all living things inspired many of the early lyrics, and William Dumbleton describes the practice of the poets, who, when they "wanted to write about time, life or some emotional or intellectual abstraction . . . often used the tree outside the door of the cottage, or the mountain down the road, or a particular waterfall nearby."[4] This practice, he explains, gives Irish poetry a sense of place richer than other literatures, like that of England, in which a writer can draw symbols from collections of cultural artifacts, such as a Grecian urn.[5] The act of naming places in a poem or story gives abstract themes a local habitation. The naming itself, the repetition of familiar words, becomes a sort of ritual and a framework for the remembering of the past.

The Celtic Literary Revival deliberately sought to reanimate the older genres in its pursuit of a national literature. The movement was born of late nineteenth-century romanticism and a struggle for independence, but it also expressed the mystical sense of Irishness, manifested in an obsessive love of the land. It was the specificity of place that rescued the art of the Celtic Revival from its tendency toward vagueness. Ann Saddlemyer remarks in "The Cult of the Celt" that the movement "possessed a strong tendency toward melancholy. . . . But the new element . . . was a sense of place, as opposed to vague atmosphere. Life and mood became more pointed by the close relationship between nature and emotion."[6] The result was a continuation of the traditional lore wherein the mystical qualities were tempered by peasant realism. The writers of the Celtic Renaissance shared a perception of the sacredness of place with the ancient Gaels, and contemporary writers still explore the nuances of local lore in their attempts to define their national identity. Such a sense of place combines tradition, legend, and history with the description of real territories. Residing in the consciousness of those touched by the island and its cultural history, it is both a personal and communal memory, a participation in the real and figurative topography of the country. Sense of place, heightened by the selectivity of art, results in a way of seeing reality from a particular vantage point. The literary landscape, thus created, has the texture of a specific region, and all the conventions of the literary genre contribute to the definition of the local color.

The question of identity, or Irishness, has been a concern of the major Irish writers of this century. It has been the dilemma plaguing critics from Daniel Corkery's *Synge and the Anglo-Irish Tradition* (1931) to George Watson's more recent work *Irish Identity and the Literary Revival* (1979), and the debate has by no means been resolved. The definition of Irishness is questioned anew as each writer faces the contradictions inherent in his relationship to his own region and to the larger world.

Although the use of landscape has been studied in fiction and poetry, "place" as a formal element has received little attention in drama studies. Leonard Lutwack, in *The Role of Place in Lit-*

erature, classifies the uses of locale in the various genres
throughout literary history; however, he says very little about
dramatic literature. He recalls that critics have dealt with "unity
of place" and with the function of certain locales in the pastoral
mode. Lutwack adds only that "place" operates differently in a
play than in other genres. Such an assertion demonstrates the
need for a study of place as a formal and thematic element in
drama. In an important contribution to this argument, Ulf Dantanus presents the relevance of the regional divisions of modern
Ireland to the development of Brian Friel as a dramatist. Dantanus discusses the significance of the political divisions between
North and South and the distinctions between Dublin and the
West as a means of understanding the playwright's work. His
method links Friel's personal experience with his themes, and
it is Dantanus's view that the dramatist's choice of forms reflects
the thematic content.[7]

Playwrights cannot describe or allude to places as directly as
writers of poetry of fiction; they must create a tangible setting
and fashion characters and speech appropriate to the locale. The
dramatic artist deals with both the fictional place of the drama
and the physical space in which the play is to be performed.
Both kinds of space can be established by stage devices such as
set, properties, music, and speech, but the world of performance
must take into account also the nature of the audience and the
theme of the story. For the purpose of this study, "place" is essentially a relationship between the artist and his audience based
on their common heritage. Like the world of the storyteller, this
is a shared context in which both parties create the place that
supports the action of the play. This approach to place proposes
a method of interpretation in which an appreciation of the formal and thematic elements of the drama flows from an understanding of the cultural identity of both the playwright and his
audience. The fundamental question is one of meaning. Certain
ways of seeing native to Irish life, when translated into drama,
can be embodied in theatrical conventions and create a specific
atmosphere and setting for the narrative.

Subjective inferences about place occur in nineteenth-century
poetry and novels where they co-exist with realistic descriptions.
The Romantic Movement gave new authority to "place" in literature. For many writers, locale became more than the setting for

human action or a symbol of some higher good; it directly influenced both character and action, and from the naturalistic settings both romanticism and realism developed. A similar
phenomenon occurred in the drama where both realistic details
and symbols evoked a metaphysical "place" as well as the locale
of the narrative.

Ibsen's *Ghosts*, for example, introduces an interaction of actor
and audience in which the physical characteristics of an actual
place both dictate and embody the theme of entrapment by the
past. The very fact of the play's being laid in Norway predisposes
the action to certain limitations. The landscape and the climate
dominate the scene and the characters; the audience, by reason
of its understanding of geography, is prepared to accept the stark
terrain, the mists, the darkness, and the yearning for the sun.
This use of place by the playwright establishes the mood of the
drama from the first curtain, particularly since the fjords impose
themselves, not as action but as an unchangeable reality. As the
play unfolds, it becomes increasingly clear to the audience that
the characters are trapped in a haunted house, irrevocably bound
by past choices as unchangeable as the gloomy landscape.

Thus the place signals the thematic context of the play, while,
at the same time, the author's choice of Norway also restricts the
interpretative range of the subject. The landscape and climate of
the northern country certainly influence the characters. Their
notions of captivity and escape are ordinarily rendered in terms
of rain and darkness and sun and warmth. Leaving Norway, going
south, is as much a determinant of the thematic structure as the
ghosts of heredity.

Strindberg's "Miss Julie" also provides a clear exposition of
the theory of place as a vehicle for interpretation. The entire play
is confined to one room. Consequently, the characters, pressured
by space, react in a more volatile manner. Their emotions seem
larger than life, and their simple actions are magnified to tragic
proportions. Beyond the kitchen is the rest of the house and the
world from which this moment has been abstracted. The tokens
of Midsummer Eve, flowers and music and dancing, form the
larger setting of the play and influence the perceptions of the audience.

The festive decorations and the music, indeed the whole magic
of the Midsummer madness, heighten the fated encounter of Jean

and Miss Julie. The excitement of the festival with its abandon-
ment of protocol—note her dancing with the retainers—is only
part of the social environment. Jean's status is made quite clear
by his livery and the riding boots, the symbols of his servitude
and the absent master. Miss Julie's father never appears on stage
but his presence controls the "place" of deportment, of social
class, of the sense of appropriateness that endures beyond the
momentary excitement of Midsummer Eve.

It is against this tradition that Miss Julie rebels, and it is her
entrapment by the same heredity and place that causes her second thoughts and her suicide. Jean provides only the occasion
for her action; in his own right, Jean is also a rebel, but his
intentions cannot surmount the reality of his servitude. He
knows that he must wait, continuing to please his master, until
the appropriate time for release with honor.

The stage setting surrounds the characters with emblems, in
the form of props, of the social milieu and the fated moment.
*"The stove is dressed with bundled branches of birch. Twigs of
juniper are scattered on the floor. On the table end stands a big
Japanese spice pot full of lilac blossoms."*[8] The flowers in the
kitchen, the view of the trees and flowers in the courtyard, and
the scent of violets on the handkerchief suggest the hope of a
good life beyond the present condition. For the cook and Jean
the future seems to hold happiness at first, and for Julie the
flowers might portend a celebration—an improvement of her sad-
dened state. The promise, however, is part of the magic of Midsummer Eve and vanishes with the morning. In the daylight,
there is the harsh reality of class consciousness, the notion that
their plan cannot succeed. The characters are bound, not by the
cramped kitchen, but by the strictures of their social status. The
symbolism of the riding boots surfaces again at the end of the
play, when the bell rings announcing the return of the master.[9]
The insistence of the bell makes Jean return to reality; his place
in the social milieu is abundantly clear to him in spite of whatever dreams he may have enjoyed during the night.

Much of this interpretation of "Miss Julie" depends upon the
audience's acceptance of the levels of "place" in the play. The
hints of social status and the restrictions that it imposes need
more than literal acknowledgment; the force of the play requires
a participation by the audience in the emotional impact. It is the

specificity of class differences which situate the drama in a certain "place" that is an historical and social milieu. It is the universal quality of entrapment which lifts the play beyond its own place and time to a permanent position in the history of dramatic literature. Thus "Miss Julie," both as literary text and theatrical moment, is not quite the same today as it was in the original production. It is the appreciation of "place" that separates the two audiences. Today, the social ambiance and the elemental magic of Midsummer Eve would be received as an historical context for the individual struggle. In its own time, the play portrayed a radical expression of the lived reality.

"Place" here, in the interaction between text and actor and actor and audience, has been described in a variety of ways. It is, most simply, a pattern of meaning that results from the cooperation of playwright and audience in the creative act. The playwright's choice of specific devices creates a physical and cultural milieu with its particular social conditions and values. The function of the audience in this exchange is very important. Either the playgoers accept, without question, the situation presented on stage, or they are aroused to recognize a conflict of values. The recognition arises from the shared experience of the playwright and audience. Consequently, the cultural landscape of a play is often more essential to a production than the physical set. Intangible as the sense of place may be, it comprises the shared vision with which the writer and spectator explore a certain piece of fiction, as well as the details of a specific locale.

Drama is both literature and performance; therefore, the methods of literary criticism alone cannot adequately describe a play. Interpretation of the text by actors and audience is also important. As in every art, the basic principle for establishing meaning in drama is the selection of details to order a particular view of reality. The mixture of arts found in a play further complicates the work of the literary critic, but the theatricality also enriches one's experience of the text. Neither the text nor the performance is more important; each has its particular artistic strength. The power in a drama derives from the audience's experience of the inner meaning, the patterns of inference that reside in the impressions created by dialogue and action.

The sense of place in drama, therefore, is part of the meaning structure and resides in the manipulation of certain stage signals

by the dramatist and their recognition by the audience. The basic
dramatic pattern—characters and situation—is the first site of
meaning in a play, and all other patterns weave in and around
the central action. The use of properties, music, and diction directs the audience to levels of inference in which the design of
inner connections can be revealed. It is in this context that the
sense of place, the power of social environment and communal
memory, operates on both the playwright and the spectator. The
idea of "place" can be both restrictive and general. It can be so
local that the drama has only regional appeal, or it can be just
specific enough to engage the spectator's imagination by its familiarity and lead the audience to participate in a view of reality
that is both particular and universal.

The audience response to a theatrical presentation defies accurate measurement, yet the value systems by which a play is
judged reside chiefly in the society from which the spectators
are drawn, just as truly as codes of behavior portrayed on stage
reflect the milieu of both playwright and audience. In this sense,
every play is regional; each playwright responds to the sense of
place, and every audience ratifies the play as "it seeks the thou-
sand compromises between the conventions of the play and the
realities of the life it knows."[10] Random signals have no place in
dramatic art. Whether the signals are direct, as in costumes,
music, properties, and verbal imagery, or whether they create a
perspective for the action by the use of space or offstage noises,
each has its own power to enhance the meaning of the play.
Each kind of signal creates its own energy and contributes to the
overall impact of the play by reinforcing the impressions made
by other signals or by creating an opposing current against which
the central motifs can be communicated.

Although music, costumes, and properties are most often used
to enhance and underline the central impression of the play, the
juxtaposition of motifs by means of these devices, prior to the
final resolution, often provides the audience with commentary
upon the action. It creates a way of seeing whereby variations in
speech and movement are carefully designed to illuminate the
dramatic meaning. This sequence of impressions comprises the
effect of theater that cannot be achieved by reading the play. Each
element is part of the pattern of meaning that can be fully realized only in performance.

The meaning which is shaped by the imagination and emotions relies in large measure upon the dramatic conventions. Although contemporary theater allows a great deal of experimentation in styles of presentation, successful playwrights continue to manipulate the conventions in order to establish rapport with the audience. Whether their choice is to follow the expected relationships of character to plot and setting or to ignore the ordinary uses of stage devices, the writers must share their particular vision of reality with the spectator. By recognizable patterns of speech or action, dramatists order the thematic and theatrical elements and bring all impressions together as a single structure of meaning.

It is these conventions—the props, characters, music, dialogue, the entire *mise en scene*—that evoke the sense of a concrete place with all the historical and cultural resonances particular to it. Devices from folklore, religion, and social tradition comprise the environment that influences the plot and characters. Any search for meaning must consider the way in which these elements cooperate in the relationship between actor and script and between actor and audience.

In Irish drama, the elusive spirit of place seems to find concrete expression most often in the peasant plays that dominated the early years of the Abbey Theatre and still exercise a significant influence over contemporary playwrights. The plays present a view of national identity that has at times served the political aspirations of Ireland and today seems to provide a frame for social commentary.

While modern Irish theater is the product of the Celtic Literary Revival of the 1890s, the peasant play also has roots in the works of Dion Boucicault. Both Synge's playboy and O'Casey's tenement dwellers are descendants of the comic rogue-heroes of his Irish plays. Boucicault was a talented man of the theater, and, although his gifts contributed more to theater management and production than to literature, his portrayal of Irish characters added a new dimension to popular drama. At the time that he wrote, the Stage Irishman had been a stock character in English drama for many years. This figure was ordinarily a stupid and unreliable character set in the subplot and playing the fool among English characters. Boucicault reversed this type by making his rogues into charming and patriotic heroes of a story in which British or Anglo-Irish characters appeared foolish. His characters are not really original; they are part of the tradition of the parasite-slave characters of the Greek and Roman theater. His making them the central characters of plays set in Ireland was innovative and extremely popular with Dublin audiences, but Boucicault's plays do not mark the true beginning of modern Irish drama. D.E.S. Maxwell observes that:

> Though their subjects and settings are Irish and their characters sentimental versions of Irish people, they are doing nothing more fundamental that adapting Irish matter to the prevailing formulas. These were not the plays to germinate a theatre expressive of lives and sensibilities whose reality had been so far unregarded by the drama.[11]

Although he chose to portray both the class in the Big House and those in the whitewashed cottages, Boucicault never grappled with social themes and the reality of Irish life. He was an entertainer, not a reformer, and much of the attractiveness of his plays resides in romantic scenery, sentimental plots, and music. The theatricality of his characters and the use of music have influenced a number of Irish writers, including John B. Keane, but at the time of the Celtic Revival, Boucicault's plays were representative of the commercial theater against which Yeats reacted. At the same time, the image of the Irishman in Boucicault's works was part of the theatrical landscape in which the Celtic Revival occurred, and the romantic view of the Irish peasantry proved stronger than the literary ideals of the founders of the National Theatre.

Actually the Irish Literary Revival is only one of the parents of the Irish National Theatre; the other was the Independent Theatre Movement already flourishing on the Continent, particularly in France and Germany. Ernest Boyd notes that the Irish Literary Theatre was a "local reaction to the prevalent stimulus, which impelled men to seek the renovations of an art abandoned to commercial speculation."[12] And it was the founders' expressed desire to create a national theater in which plays of artistic quality and Irish interest would be performed. The shared vision, recorded by Lady Gregory in *Our Irish Theatre*, was not as single-minded as her memoir suggests. There were among the founders several views of the nature of a national literature, but, regardless of their differences of interpretation, "the ground that was most immediately common to all the four founders of the Irish Literary Theatre was the desire to produce plays that were different from, and better than, the stereotyped drama of the commercial theatre."[13]

One of the valuable exercises in reading the history of the first ten years of the movement is to trace the emergence of national identity and popular concerns in the dramatic offerings. A vital part of the imaginative adventure was the use of distinctively Irish material in both the poetic and realistic plays. Directed by Yeats to the Aran Islands, Synge turned from Continental influences to Irish themes, and his "In The Shadow of the Glen" and "Riders to the Sea" set examples of excellence and style that both writers and actors strove to emulate.

A listing of the plays from the first ten years of the dramatic movement shows both a variety of themes and a growing focus on rural settings and plots. There are plays based on the heroic tales, such as Alice Milligan's *The Last Feast of the Fianna*, folk stories like Yeats's "The Pot of Broth," and patriotic symbols like his "Cathleen ni Houlihan." The most frequently recurring themes, however, depict peasant life. Brenda Katz Clarke suggests that the Dublin audiences, only recently removed from the land, regarded the Irish peasant as a symbol of national identity. She concludes that:

> The peasant play became the vehicle of national expression because the poetic plays which dealt with myth and saga were too distant from the immediate questions of land ownership and home rule. The Land War had always been an intrinsic part of the repeal movement, and plays like Colum's *The Land* appealed to nationalistic audiences. A national theatre must be popular and the peasant play met the requirements of that demand.[14]

Observing the development of the rural themes is particularly enlightening. Not only do the peasant dramas center on the hearth, the figurative and actual heart of the rural Irish home, but situations, reflecting concerns with inheritance, marriage, and emigration, also recur as subjects for the plays. Like the hearth, the land is a central motif in the Irish Literary Revival and, along with religious and political self-determination, becomes a recurring motif of Irish identity in the Abbey plays.

These subjects were topical in the early days of the dramatic movement; today, the first ten years of the Abbey Theatre give clues to the meaning of plays in which the same themes are employed by contemporary dramatists.

The early plays create a native Irish drama both through native themes and also through attention to language. Each of the early playwrights approached the matter of language in different ways. Lady Gregory grew up with an interest in the stories told by her nurse, Mary Sheridan, and "place," as Hazard Adams comments, "gave her the Kiltartan dialect in which she wrote nearly all her works. It was around her in her childhood and she kept connections with it through her local marriage and her continued residence at Coole."[15] Lady Gregory's dramatic models were the farces of Moliere, but her particular gift was her talent for languages and the sensitivity with which she approached the native dialects of Galway. The result of her attention to language and rural situations was effective characterization in which her sense of place and event was delineated by the dialogue. In addition, Lady Gregory's dedication to the collecting of folklore and her interest in the Kiltartan townspeople provided her with a repertoire of characters. Not only farmers were represented in her plays, but also clerks and magistrates, policemen and workhouse inmates, fugitives from the law and gossips—every class except the Ascendancy. Her first play was produced in 1903, and while "Twenty-Five" is not often remembered as one of her important works, it marked the beginning of a very productive decade in her life and in the history of the National Theatre.

Lady Gregory's "Spreading the News" shared the bill for the opening of the new theater in Lower Abbey Street with Yeats's Cuchullain play "On Baile's Strand." The comedy, originally intended as a nostalgic piece about a girl's loss of her good name, appeared as the story of hen-pecked Bartley Fallon, who takes a sentimental joy in his own bad fortune and becomes the "murderer" in the tale. In "Spreading the News," as in all her comedies, Lady Gregory situates universal conditions within the lifestyle of Galway peasants. Her most successful characters embrace a wide range of social types, and her ear for the sentence patterns of those English-speakers who think in Irish gives general human nature a local dialect.

Critics are divided on whether Lady Gregory's Kiltartan dialect provided a model for her contemporaries or whether her work was simply imitative. What really matters here is that she, along with Yeats and Synge, set the pace for later playwrights. Even if the force of her personality and her managerial skills were the only causes for praise, she was a considerable force in the shaping of the Abbey Theatre through her share in the directorship.

Although Lady Gregory had strong nationalist sympathies, it was never her expressed desire to dabble in politics; still, her play "The Rising of the Moon" can be read as a political parable. The story of the fugitive who stimulated pronationalist sentiments in the conscience of a police sergeant certainly emphasizes the political divisions in Ireland. It demonstrates, too, the very dualities in the Irish nature which Sean O'Faolain describes in his study *The Irish*. Needless to say, both the officials at Dublin Castle and the nationalist Sinn Fein found fault with this play. The Castle refused to lend uniforms to the Abbey because the management apparently endorsed the play's suggestion that a representative of the Crown could be moved by the Irish cause. The nationalists complained that the drama showed a policeman in a favorable light. In *Our Irish Theatre*, Lady Gregory agrees that the story has an historical setting, easily recognizable in Irish life, yet she asserts that the real conflict in the short play is in the mind of the police sergeant. It is the struggle between his present and his past, between his duty and his sympathies, not an illustration of the Irish-English controversy.[16]

"The Rising of the Moon," like "Spreading the News," manages to situate the scene in a specific Irish setting through the medium of language. The former draws on the memory of a well-known rebel song for the context of the play. The setting is sparse, the mere suggestion of a pier at night, yet the repetition of the song fills out the wider scope of the scene and its probable history. The nationalist motif of the song, juxtaposed with the conversation of the ballad-singer and the sergeant, both reveals and hides the identity of the fugitive. The audience never doubts that the man is either the "wanted" outlaw or one of his confederates; only the policeman seems not to recognize the signs around him. Here the sense of place is projected through the use of dialect and music. The shared experience of the original audiences, to whom the subject was certainly more topical than it would be today, immediately created a rapport between the actors and the spectators. Even in present experience, which is not so acutely attuned to the politics of the turn of the century, the sense of Ireland and the aura of distrust between officials and the nameless singer are evident from the beginning. The repeated musical motif creates an emotional current that alerts the audience to the psychological stress and the political meaning.

"Spreading the News," in contrast, suggests the village fair through posters and a few makeshift booths. Again, in this play, it is not the scenery that creates the place, but the repertoire of characters. To the fair come all the representatives of village life: those who sell their produce, those who come to buy, and those who keep the peace. As in all rural societies, the fair is a major activity; it is the scene of both business and social transactions. Consequently, the confusion which results from Mrs. Tarpey's misunderstanding of the words she only partially hears creates both the humor of the play and a view of local life. The magistrate's attitude is typical of the Anglo-Irish distaste for the native Irish. He embodies the distrust and the sense of superiority with which the English landlords regarded their Irish tenants, and the reactions of the villagers to the story of the "murder" run the gamut from disbelief to elaborate reconstructions of the causes and effects of Bartley's action. The result is a vivid picture of Irish village life.

In the same year as Lady Gregory's debut as a playwright, the first plays of John Millington Synge and Padraic Colum were produced by the Irish National Theatre Society. Although they came from different backgrounds and had different literary gifts, each of these writers contributed to establishing the peasant play as an Abbey tradition. Synge became the outstanding talent in the Irish theater, and Colum, from a Midlands farming family, provided the true beginning of peasant realism in the theater. Both enjoyed only brief careers at the Abbey: Synge because of his untimely death, and Colum because he left the company at the time of the *Playboy* controversy and eventually emigrated to America. In just a few years, their plays created a pattern for success known even today as the "Abbey" play.

Synge's association with the National Theatre Society began with the production of "In the Shadow of the Glen." This play was as important to the future of the young society as Miss Horni-

man's offer of a permanent home for the company, which occurred in the same year. The one-act play demonstrated Synge's
grasp of the peasant idiom. It also evoked stormy protests from
those who objected to his portrayal of Irish peasant life. Synge's
characterization of the wife, who chose a romantic existence
with a tramp over loyalty to her husband, was attacked as a smear
on the nation's honor. The dramatist's success in this play, as in
others, is his depiction of the loneliness of life in the remote
mountain regions of the West. The folk motif of the husband's
trick and the wife's reversal of the expected behavior are grimly
humorous devices which highlight the human frustration generated by loneliness and the confinement of social conventions.
George Watson states in his study of national identity among the
Anglo-Irish writers that Synge "clearly dramatizes the connections between the monotonous loneliness and the prevalence of
heavy drinking and even insanity, as well as a sort of compensat-
ing relish for violent deeds."[17] It was such unvarnished observations of the Irish rural scene which resulted in the protests by
those whose illusions of Irish character he had assaulted. Even
the Irish people themselves had grown accustomed to the stage
nationalism of Dion Boucicault where the patriotism of the men
and the purity of the women set the Irish peasantry apart from
the English and Anglo-Irish landlords. In "In the Shadow of the
Glen," Synge was accused of deliberately attacking the national
character, an accusation which would become a loud protest over
his *Playboy of the Western World,* his greatest contribution to
the peasant genre.

The *Playboy of the Western World* portrays a society of men
and women in whose lives the elements of tragedy and comedy
are closely mingled, and it was the realism with which the play
was written that caused the outcry at its first production. Some
critics concluded that Synge's play slandered the people of Mayo
by suggesting that they would consider patricide an heroic deed.
The early audiences failed to recognize that Synge was actually
satirizing the Irish preference for illusions over reality.

The play concerns Christy Mahon who unexpectedly appears
in a country public house with the tale of how he killed his
father. The villagers seem to be old men, women, and the ineffectual Shawn Keogh. In such company, Christy finds himself a hero,
and, as he rises in the esteem of the peasants, he stands a good

chance of successfully wooing Pegeen Mike, the daughter of the publican. At the end, Old Mahon appears in his bloody bandages, and the hero is dethroned. Although the plot seems romantic, Synge's treatment of the facts and his view of peasant life are bluntly realistic. He manages to capture the peasants' distrust of the authorities as well as their skill in eliciting information from strangers by the art of indirect questions.

Synge's language, valued for its vitality, color, and exuberance, contributes to the reality of his characters and situations and stands as his legacy to Irish drama. But while he is undoubtedly the greatest of the Irish playwrights, Lady Gregory and Padraic Colum probably had an even greater formative influence on the younger dramatists who continued the folk tradition in the theater.

If, today, Padraic Colum is heard of less than Lady Gregory or Synge, in the first decade of the dramatic movement it seemed that he was destined to be a major playwright. He was the youngest writer associated with the Abbey Theatre, and he seemed to possess from the beginning a mature theatrical talent. Colum studied the works of Ibsen and the European masters of realism. His first success *Broken Soil* demonstrates his gift for re-creating Irish scenes, characters, and dialogue. Later revised and renamed *The Fiddler's House*, the play probably deserves to be listed as the true beginning of realistic drama in Ireland. The protagonist, Con Hourican, is a farmer who prefers the open road and an audience for his fiddling to the duties of the farm. Con's attitude causes strain and division in his family and misunderstanding among the townspeople. Ultimately, one of his daughters sympathizes with him and joins his wandering life, while the other girl settles down on the farm. Colum, like Synge, presents the artist as outcast in the rural society, but, unlike Synge, he was more at home with the characteristic response of the peasantry to the outsider. Boyd offers the portrayal of the "distrust entertained by respectable peasants towards the unattached man of the roads" as an illustration of the playwright's difference in handling the theme.[18] The reaction of Con Hourican's daughters and neighbors differs greatly from the welcome Christy Mahon receives in *Playboy*. Synge focuses on the mystique of the man outside the law while Colum presents the normal fears that settled folk have of the wanderer.

Colum wrote two major plays in addition to *The Fiddler's House*—*The Land* and *Thomas Muskerry*. All three mark him as a significant force in the formative years of the Irish Theatre. *The Land* dramatizes the conflict between a generation which had struggled to own its small farms and a younger generation to whom the call of the larger world had great appeal. The play reflects a reality in Irish rural life. Once the Land Act of 1903 had finally been passed, the people who had fought so hard found themselves alone on the land. Their children had emigrated in search of greater economic opportunities and personal freedom. These two plays made Padraic Colum extremely popular with the Abbey Theatre audiences. Because he was a Roman Catholic who came from the same rural conditions that he was portraying, he was the kind of writer who seemed to fulfill the audience's expectations of a national theater.

Both Synge and Colum explore the possibilities of the peasant genre; Synge transcends the routine to touch universal qualities, while Colum realistically interprets ordinary characters and events. It was this realism, as well as the language of the simple plays, that attracted many of the younger dramatists to the works of Colum and Lady Gregory. For years, writers of comedy managed to fill the Abbey seats for performance after performance and secured for the rural plays the designation "Abbey plays."

In the context of the peasant tradition, one must mention also the plays of George Fitzmaurice in spite of his very little recognition from the Abbey and the rest of the world. His output includes comedy, tragedy, and fantasy; his peasantry is true to life and his dialogue rich in idioms strongly influenced by Gaelic. Austin Clarke notes in his introduction to the dramatic fantasies that Fitzmaurice's language, drawn from his native Kerry, is akin to the rhythmic speech of Synge. "It has in it the rapid rhythm of Kerry Irish and it seems to catch its pace from those fantastically long place-names which one finds in the 'Kingdom'"[19] Fitzmaurice never wrote prefaces to his plays; therefore, critics can only infer that he attempted to reproduce a language that was close to the Gaelic original.

The plays of Lady Gregory, Synge, Colum, and Fitzmaurice shape the rural speech of four distinct sections of Ireland into a literary medium. Only in Synge, however, does this language reach poetic heights; the others create a theatrical language closer to the actual dialects. Their plays demonstrate the dramatic possibilities of peasant life, and they prepare the way for the dramatists who would make the rural drama into an Abbey formula for success.

The preoccupation with re-creating the regional dialects as well as the subjects important to the rural communities set up a new stereotype on the Irish stage, a romantic view of the Irish peasant. Thus, the realism of the early playwrights shifted toward a false ideal that linked patriotism with virtue, and, ultimately, interfered with the production of experimental plays. In recent years, playwrights are rediscovering the genuine sense of place partly as a result of the forming of the Amateur Drama Council. This organization has given formal direction to amateur groups by sponsoring festivals. Increasingly, the regional theaters have enriched Irish drama by their experimentation, and the annual Dublin Theatre Festival has both produced foreign plays and encouraged new plays by Irish dramatists. Some regional playwrights, like John B. Keane, have brought a new dimension to the rural play by expressing the struggle between tradition and contemporary life.

Spirit of place is important to Irish literature because it expresses the national character. It is important to contemporary Irish drama, in particular, because it is the spiritual and cultural milieu behind the *mise en scene*. Therefore, concentration on the meanings inherent in the choice of physical details and characters in twentieth-century plays reveals subtle modulations of intention which color the use of traditional Irish themes. Modern life is marked by change and mobility. Technology and mass communication have eroded the individual differences that once characterized nations and places. Some attempts at preserving the past have made tourist attractions out of cultural heritage. For this reason, discussion of place in the drama of John B. Keane must make clear at the beginning that it is not another attempt at rescuing an elusive past from the erosion of modern times. It is essential to recall that the landscape is both physical and temporal and that one's native land includes not only a geographic location but also the emotional, intellectual, and spiritual connections with an environment. This sense of belonging to a particular place and time endures in spite of the effects of technology and mobility. These are the ties of family and culture that Catherine Middleton suggests keep an individual rooted in a certain place. She adds that if the person does move away "the features of the landscape, compounded of so many different elements, will continue to affect the way he thinks, feels and acts. This place, experienced in the past, will become a reference point against which all his subsequent experiences of place are measured."[20] This is the case with James Joyce whose entire literary output concerns the land he had left as a young man. His sense of Dublin not only bound him to his past but also influenced the distinctive qualities of his writing. In the same way, place functions in contemporary Irish drama as a legitimate tool in recreating realistic human situations.

John B. Keane is a successor to the peasant playwrights of the Celtic Literary Revival who demonstrates the vitality of the sense of place in contemporary literature. The age-old themes do not change much in Ireland, but Keane's angle of vision shifts from the political interests of the earlier period to concern for the individual within the system. Both his own experience and his understanding of the expectations of his audience color Keane's articulation of the landscape of the soul against the backdrop of Kerry. He appears to have made peace with the "genius of the place" since his plays are both genuinely folk and modern at the same time. It is his skill at delineating the twentieth-century malaise in western Ireland that makes Keane an important regional writer. His astute observations on human nature also give a universal dimension to his portrayal of life in a small town.

Place, then, functions as a formal and thematic element in Keane's dramas. Authentic characters, music, and language provide realistic details that evoke the North Kerry landscape; these same conventions comprise a frame of reference for the thematic concerns of the plot. Traditional characters juxtaposed with contemporary issues result in the dual thrust of nostalgia and criticism that marks his plays.

3

Dramatic Devices and the Sense of Place

The early plays of John B. Keane are safely within the tradition
of the Irish peasant drama. Consequently, the cottage settings
and his inclination toward melodrama have sometimes caused
the Dublin critics to disregard his plays as imitative exercises of
a beginning playwright. Although the early plays are certainly
more derivative than the later ones, they nevertheless provide a
strong case for the use of conventions as signals of the spirit of
place, and, in particular, a sense of the West of Ireland.

The wild beauty of the West of Ireland is apparent both in his
characters and in the elemental violence that seethes just below
the surface of the plays and bursts the restraints of civilized
behavior when the action requires it. This is the reality of Kerry
which is often misunderstood by the critics of Keane's plays.
Robert Hogan observes in *After the Irish Renaissance*:

> He is sometimes accused of being a latterday Boucicault whose plays
> are faultily constructed and harmed by large injections of melo-
> drama. However, Dublin critics are little more aware of what life is
> like in Clare and Kerry than New York critics are familiar with life
> in Nebraska and Georgia. Keane is not really larger than life, but life
> in Kerry is larger than life in Dublin.[1]

Certainly, exaggerated characters frequently signal melodrama,
but, as Hogan suggests, the larger issue of Keane's relationship
to Irish melodrama is more complex than one might expect. *Sive*
certainly has some melodramatic elements, the most obvious
being the familiar device of the letter; however, the play itself is
a tragicomic portrayal of rural life. It may depend upon certain
types from the Kerry countryside for its emotional power, but it
is not a play in which the issues can be stated in black and
white. Once such ambiguities occur, and one finds fewer moral

absolutes among twentieth-century audiences, the play cannot be classified as melodrama.

Keane's debt to Irish melodrama is evident in his use of music to reinforce the emotion of the plays and in a certain heightening and simplification of characters to present a world recognizable to his audience. His plays, however, are concerned more with character than with plot, and, in this regard, they are descendants of the realistic theater. In an article, "A Last Instalment," John B. Keane defends melodramatic devices for their theatricality and suggests "that critics have made melodrama the poor relation of the legitimate theatre," and that they have "derided it and held it up as something to be ashamed of."[2]

This study will not develop a case for melodrama as a genre in modern Irish theater; however, it is important to recognize that references to Keane's work as melodramatic or regional are intended to describe his methods, not to render a judgment.

John B. Keane's work is regional in the best sense. It evokes his relationship with a particular place and a particular people in whom he recognizes a microcosm of modern Ireland. The playwright lives in a small town. It is a busy town, and, walking through the streets with Keane as guide, one can begin to grasp the vitality of its contrasts as well as the peace of its comparative isolation. The River Feale winds between a ruined castle and the racetrack, and the outline of a modern dairy complex shares the skyline with the spires of the churches. These contrasts illustrate the point that it is about modern Kerry that Keane is writing, but the people still retain the gift of leisurely conversation that urban settings have lost. Keane remarked during a radio interview that when he has urgent business it is necessary for him to travel the back streets or he would never reach his destination.[3] This writer's visits to Listowel have confirmed this view; the talk of the people was lively, anecdotal, and full of unhurried attention to the listener. Keane's plays, too, have much of this spirit of community, and he shares the Westerner's sense of right which is often independent of the legal system. It is this law of community that selects and arranges the perceptions of order in his plays. While a sense of belonging to a specific community can best be realized in the interaction of characters, the audience can perceive it also in the stage set and the descriptions of the environment provided in the dialogue. The sense of place is embodied first of all in representations of local landscape and the social milieu depicted by the cottage setting.

The cottage kitchen was the traditional setting of the Irish folk play. William G. Fay describes the realism with which the early stage sets were constructed; he notes that even the dimensions of the sets exactly reproduced the cottages of the west of Ireland.[4] The cottage interior became the trademark of the Abbey production, and while the stage dimensions changed through the years, the characteristics of the kitchen sets did not. The early works of Keane continue the tradition of the cottage setting; the farms portrayed in his plays conform both to the theatrical expectations and to the conditions of rural Ireland in the mid-twentieth century. The farms tend to be small, under thirty acres, and are usually described in terms of the number of cows the acreage can support. The cottage, the hearth, is the focus of the life of the country people, and, while certain differences will express a farmer's prosperity, the farmhouses are essentially the same. Stage directions would not need to be explicit; the designation "cottage" could have only one interpretation, and Conrad Arensberg describes such a farmhouse:

> It was a white-washed stone cottage, rectangular, roofed with slate (though it was only a few years ago that they gave up thatch). Its long sides faced roughly north and south each with a door opening directly out into the yards. In the gable of the roof was a loft for sleeping; otherwise it was confined to a single story. The central room, the largest by far, was the kitchen. There the family passed their lives and prepared and ate the food cooked on the hearth. The hearth was an open turf fire, built in a chimney large enough to have two hobs or seats deep within on either side. It had, too, an iron hook which swung the cookingpots out into the room from the fire.[5]

Behind the hearth was another room; in many houses in the poorer regions, this "west room" would be the only room other than the kitchen and the loft. In some houses, however, there is another room, usually a bedroom, at the opposite end of the kitchen. The kitchen, which opens out on the haggard or farmyard, is the center of life on an Irish farm; even the men, who work in the garden and the fields, spend a good portion of their time near the house and yard.[6]

When John B. Keane reproduces the cottage on stage, he introduces his audience to conditions in North Kerry. The remoteness of the villages and farms, suggested by stage directions or dialogue, reinforces the isolation of the rural West from the mainstream of modern Ireland. In such sequestered settings time seems to stand still. Although the author situates the dramatic action in the present, the attitudes and social conditions portrayed seem better suited to the nineteenth-century theater. The cottage settings appear primitive to modern understanding, and the characters are occupied with activities and problems that could be thought old-fashioned. Yet Keane reminds the audience that the time is the present or the recent past. It is the place that creates the sense of distance. Therefore, one must either receive the action as the representation of an earlier period or realize that Keane's remote settings are accurate reproductions of the rural scene in Ireland as late as the 1950s. This capacity to inspire a dual response is the strength of Keane's plays and the whole focus of concern with the spirit of place. This is the quality of place that reproduces the traditional expectations and allows contemporary characters to clash with the spiritual and historical contexts of their lives. This, too, is the source both of Keane's popularity at home and the misunderstanding of his plays abroad.

The physical settings of the early plays circumscribe the activity of the character within the limited space of the rural cottage. Some of the scenes also suggest a wider prospect. In *Sharon's Grave*, the stage directions require that the rugged and wild coastline be visible through the open door and window (SG 311). As in Ibsen, the craggy headland is both setting and symbol; the deep hole and the legendary Sharon are as central to the realistic situation as the white horses and the mill race of *Rosmersholm*. Keane immediately draws attention beyond the cottage interior to the external forces threatening the security of the household. In the first act of *Sharon's Grave*, the wild scenery in the background juxtaposed with the stillness of the deathbed scene disposes the audience to look for some invasion of the peace.

Keane here employs a commonplace of the theater—the arrival of the stranger. In *Sharon's Grave* the traveler, whose arrival begins the action, proves to be an obliging neighbor, and the "outsider" is a member of the family. It is Dinzie Conlee, a nephew to the dying man, who threatens the peace of the cottage as he schemes to deprive his cousins of their inheritance. The problem of the ownership of land is a well-known theme in Irish literature; in this play it is associated with physical and psychological distortions and the sterility of unhealthy sexuality.

Some of the characters, notably Neelus and Dinzie, are grotesque in mind and body. Neelus, the son of the house, is emotionally handicapped and as sterile as the bleak landscape because of his unnatural preoccupation with the woman of his imagination, but he has a gentle spirit which evokes sympathy. In contrast, his cousin Dinzie is distorted in body and soul. His disposition, warped because of his physical incapacity, is essentially cruel and selfish. His chief concern is his ambition for his cousins' land so that, having property, he may attract some woman to marry him. *Sharon's Grave* has the potential, then, of representing two levels of meaning in its stage setting, as the barren land-forms in the distance brood over the cottage interior. Eventually, as the spectators become aware of the legend of the beautiful Sharon and her ugly servant, the locale and the folk tale merge to represent the psychological states of the characters.

A similar use of the backcloth occurs in *The Year of the Hiker*. Here, the open window and porch door reveal a view of fields and mountains, suggesting, as the drama unfolds, the call of the road. The freedom of the fields and hills provides a contrast to the confinement of the house and the routine of the farm. The opening scene makes very clear that the residents of the farmhouse resent the absence of the head of the house and his apparent unwillingness to shoulder responsibility. Freda's remark sets the tone of the play and emphasizes the division between the freedom of the road and the stability and security of the farm:

> It's in the blood . . . a constant calling to be up and away. No sense of responsibility, wife and family all forgotten when the humour catches them. Didn't you ever see birds migrating? Well, like the birds or fish, these people get uneasy and restless when their time for moving comes. It's a disease—like tuberculosis or pneumonia. Wandering is God's curse! (Hiker 17)

The dichotomy of place is distinctly drawn in this speech and in all the dialogue of act 1. As the family speaks of the Hiker and his selfish irresponsibility, the vista beyond the cottage underlines their words and actions.

Then, Hiker Lacey returns. The audience has been prepared for his entrance by the references to his failures and the fear that he will return and spoil Mary's wedding day. His appearance, however, is quiet and somewhat sad; Hiker Lacey is a tired, old man. His arrival triggers a reversal in the sympathies of the audience. The "long-suffering" maiden aunt receives him so unkindly—his appearance of weakness and need contrasts sharply with her reproving tone—that the audience might wonder whether its original assessment was accurate. The entrance of the "stranger" is, of course, the real beginning of the play. The interplay of attitudes in the setting of a secure cottage and against the backdrop of the open road creates a new angle of vision. No longer is the contrast between duty and irresponsibility so clearly cut as the opening scene suggests. The physical contrasts of landscape and cottage become symbols for the attitudinal and social constraints that are the real source of the conflict.

Keane does not employ the device of the double vista in all his rural dramas; in most cases, the world outside the cottage must be introduced by the speech of the characters in association with the audience's perception of the real Irish landscape. The audience depends on the characters' references to other times, places, and external circumstances in order to establish a context for the motives and actions of the play. Keane's first play, Sive, manages to combine the melodramatic aspects of Kerry with the economic reality of rural life in modern Ireland. The central motif is not only the "selling" of a young woman in an arranged marriage but also the family conflicts occasioned by the changing times.

Sive, an orphan, is an attractive eighteen-year-old girl who lives with her maternal grandmother and an uncle and his wife. The tensions in the Glavin household are evident from the first lines, and the limitations of the small cottage kitchen magnify the domestic conflict. The cottage has two functions in this play, as in others: it localizes the action, and it forces the situation to explode since the characters, confined both by the cottage walls and social expectations, have no other outlet. Sive's ignorance of her illegitimate birth heightens the tensions; therefore, both her education and the arranged marriage seem to present ways out of poverty for the girl. However, allusions to her mother's misfortune and her father's death by drowning also suggest the direction of her life.

Although the landscape surrounding the Glavin cottage is neither specified in the stage directions nor glimpsed through the window, the text emphasizes both the remoteness of the house from the village and the uncertainty of the terrain. At Sive's first appearance, she explains that her lateness in returning from school was caused by a puncture in the bicycle tire. She says: "I was lucky to meet the master on the road. He gave me a lift as far as the end of the bohareen" (S 12). Not only is the Glavin cottage a distance from the village, but the dialogue emphasizes that it is also removed from the main road and only accessible by a narrow lane. The length of the trip and the difficulty of the terrain are referred to several times in the first act. Even the dangers of walking at night are mentioned by Thomasheen Rua: "But think of the dark, girl, and the phuca (pauses) the mad, red eyes of him like coals of fire lighting in his head. There is no telling what you would meet on a dark road" (S 40). The matchmaker's primary reason for the warning is to frighten Sive into accepting Sean Dota as a companion on her errand. Thomasheen's concern is for the marriage bargain more than for her safety, but his words, along with the other references to distance, help to create the sense of remoteness and the unpredictability of the elements.

The terrain is not only sparsely settled, but also surrounded by bog, where Mike Glavin has been cutting turf. In the first act, Mike leaves the house in anger after he and Mena disagree over the marriage contract. Mena follows him, and Liam Scuab, arriving at the cottage, remarks that "they've gone away over the bog" (S 30). Later that same evening, Sive is sent to borrow equipment for transporting the newly cut turf (S 39). Both of these allusions, apparently incidental to the narrative, establish the proximity of the bog to the cottage. These details announce to an Irish audience specific physical conditions, and the playwright counts on their recognizing the spongy and uncertain surface of the bog and the danger of losing one's footing, especially in the holes left after the turf has been cut. Based on the subsequent events of the plot, these references to the terrain foreshadow Sive's fate as well as ordinary concerns of the villagers. Toward the end of the play, when the girl cannot be found in the house, the bog is perceived as her most likely route of escape:

> Mena. What if she fell into a hole. . . .
> Mike. I'll get a lantern in the stable—my waders!
> Thomasheen. I will go with you. There's danger in the holes at night, not knowing the minute you'd slip from a high bank. (S 107–8)

These are normal reactions, but, in the context of *Sive*, they also emphasize the consistent danger of the environment. The bog functions in much the same way as the cottage. Both are familiar places carrying connotations of specific physical and economic conditions. Both sites become a frame of recognizable reality within which the action of the play can proceed.

In *The Highest House on the Mountain*, the familiar landscape suggests a dual vision. The house of the title is not the setting for the action, but, like the steeple of *The Master Builder* or the orphanage in *Ghosts*, it is a symbol of the spiritual reality of the play. The scene is laid in the kitchen of a farmhouse in the Southwest of Ireland; the time is winter. The remoteness of the farm is suggested both by references to the main road (HH 2) and to the attitudes of mountainy men (HH 7). The brothers Mike and Sonny are well paired with their respective houses. The farmhouse is Mike's and he, although lonely and decidedly conservative in his values and judgments, is apparently normal in his relations with other persons. His brother, who has his own house on the mountain, even more isolated than the setting of the play, is silent and withdrawn and suffers from an unnamed "hurt." He is reluctant to have his solitude disturbed by the arrival of his nephew's new wife.

The house on the mountain, at first, seems to be a symbol for the hurt and the isolation of Sonny. Then it becomes evident that all the characters in the play are hurting. It is only when Sonny and Julie reach out to each other in kindness and genuine concern that the highest house becomes a kind of paradise (HH 64) and a chance for a new beginning (HH 64–65). The house is never a symbol of perfection, but it offers to those who are open to love, namely Sonny and Julie, a chance to salvage something from their pain.

This duality, where the foreground is either played against an opposing backdrop or the visible scene and consistently refers to something outside of or beyond the present, is a reflection both of the Pagan-Christian strains in the Irish character and of the quest for national identity in the modern world. This is not to suggest that John B. Keane intends to produce symbolic drama. The fact is that he has no pretensions to such a role; however, in portraying Irish life as he observes it, Keane has caught both the strengths and weaknesses of modern Ireland, and even his cottage settings can illustrate the tensions.

Even more explicit referents of place than the cottage, the characters of Keane's early plays clearly establish a west of Ireland locale. Matchmakers, tinkers and other travelers bring to the dramas certain character types specifically identified with the landscape of the Gaeltacht.

The outsider occupies a unique place in Irish culture because the rural districts constitute a closed, self-contained society in which any stranger arouses curiosity and suspicion. The distrust of strangers extends even to returning emigrants and to familiar figures such as matchmakers and tinkers. There are two traditions in Irish literature. The first treats the outsider as a deliverer from oppression or poverty. The stranger, in this case, could be a landowner or a returning Yank. Here the figure of the outsider fulfills the folk expectations of prosperity, wealth, or political influence which will release the townland from its crisis. This is, of course, the Celtic myth of the god-hero returning to deliver his people in a time of emergency. This is the story of Arthur's return from Avalon and the persistent legend that Parnell had not really died. In this context, the stranger/outsider is a source of salvation as the character of the Countess Cathleen in Yeats's play can illustrate.

The same play also dramatizes the other view of the stranger, that of the outsider who disrupts the tranquility of the village and whose arrival portends disaster and suffering. In "The Countess Cathleen," the merchants are strangers and viewed with suspicion, although their wealth offers the people a way of avoiding starvation. The "outsiders" in this instance represent foreign political power as well as forces alien to the Catholic Church, that is, the traditional enemies of Irish values. Yeats described his play as a morality play, which suggests that his characters achieve an allegorical significance in the realms of politics or religion. The possible interpretations would be readily accessible to an audience familiar with Irish history.

The stranger or outsider in contemporary Irish plays is less obviously a symbol of political or religious allegiance. The playwrights do employ local characters, music, and customs in order to create a sense of traditional values. These elements serve as a reminder of the received beliefs, and against the backdrop of similar cultural deposits and shared experience dramatists set modern attitudes and problems. As a result, the conflict in a contemporary play is often the individual's struggle with opposing value systems rather than the national concerns of the early Irish theater.

Keane's *Sive* provides a good example of opposing attitudes in contemporary Ireland. The play is laid in the 1950s in rural Ireland. The major characters represent three generations of the Glavin family and a corresponding range of ideas. From the beginning, the sympathy of the audience is divided, not as one might expect between the old and the new, but between spiritual and material concerns. The economic realities that control the central conflict could belong to any literature; it is Keane's use of regional characters to articulate his values that makes *Sive* an Irish play.

The realistic drawing of the characters results from Keane's careful attention to the details of daily routine. First, the prevalence of Irish words in the dialogue suggests that these characters are part of a society not far removed from the time when Irish was the common language. Second, the sense of authenticity appears even in the stage business that the playwright gives his characters. The opening of *Sive*, where Nanna Glavin is sitting at the fire with her pipe and Mena is making bread, accurately evokes a scene replayed in every Irish kitchen. The precise directions for Mena's actions are typical of the care Keane takes to depict realistically the Kerry in which he lives. By recreating ordinary Irish life so faithfully, he provides a frame of reference in which the action of the play can develop. In the same way, all the minor characters of *Sive* have a vibrant life. Robert Hogan notes that in many realistic plays the minor characters are only stereotypes employed for purposes of the plot; however, the small roles in Keane's play are faithful to life, and, "heightened by just a touch of grotesqueness," each is a convincing individual.[7]

Matchmakers and tinkers are native to the Kerry landscape, and, in *Sive*, they function as elements both of setting and plot. As setting, the characters provide the flavor of the Southwest. They are so much out of step with modern conditions that they seem to be remnants from the past, yet their presence not only heightens the pace of the drama but also situates the narrative in a specific place. Thomasheen Sean Rua, the matchmaker, widens the preexisting gap between Nanna and Mena Glavin. There is a perverse twist to his approach to the younger woman. Although he represents an ancient custom, totally foreign to the contemporary idea of marriage, he is able to bring Mena to consider his bargain. In spite of her realistic outlook on most topics and her firsthand knowledge of the challenges facing a woman in marriage, Mena agrees to the match. The success of his appeal strongly underscores the spiritual-material struggle in the play.

The character of Thomasheen jolts the audience's perceptions. Those who had developed a sympathy for the old ways, by noting Mena's treatment of her mother-in-law, now recognize that there are flaws in that judgment. Thomasheen has entered the enclosed world of the cottage, and, although he is not really a stranger, he has instigated the central action of the play. He has forced the audience to take sides. One may have sympathies for Nanna, another for Mena, but, with the entrance of the matchmaker, all realize that it is Sive who will suffer because she is caught between the two. The matchmaker, then, forces the hidden conflicts of the cottage to materialize as actions. While he provides a bit of local color and humor, even in the 1950s Thomasheen Sean Rua would have represented a dying tradition. His function in the play, apart from his catalytic influence on the plot, is to establish clearly a bond of shared memory between the playwright and the audience. Having created such a bond, the matchmaker generates in the audience the real tensions between heritage and modernity in Ireland as well as the fictional tensions of the drama.

The tinker Pats Bocock and his musical son portray even more vividly the power of the outsider in an enclosed society. Their entrances participate in the age-old rituals grounded in hospitality and superstition. At the same time, the household also illustrates contemporary attitudes of the settled community toward the travelers. The tinkers provide a glimpse of the genuine atmosphere of rural Kerry as they make the accustomed rounds, begging for their sustenance in homes where they have been kindly received at other times. Pats Bocock is known in the Glavin cottage as his words to Nanna indicate (S 52). There is a mixture of familiarity and cajoling speech in his greeting to both Nanna and Mena, since he realizes that it is the woman of the house who will determine the success of their begging. There is a certain reticence in the asking; they request only enough food for the day, always in the hope of receiving a gift of money:

> No more than a dorn of sugar and a dusteen of tea. We have the caravan abeyant in the steam-rolled road. Liam Scuab *(He bends his head in thanks while Carthalawn stands rigid)*, a dacent man, gave us the side of a loaf. We have our own accutarements. If there is the giving of tea and sugar we will thank the hand that gives it. If there is not, maybe there is the giving of a silver piece. Is there anything from Thomasheen Sean Rua of the mountain—making it in plenty he is. (S 52)

Their begging only intensifies the dissension between Nanna and Mena. The old woman immediately gets up to give them the tea and sugar; Mena stops her, and she is abetted in her refusal by Thomasheen's abusive language. The old woman, silenced because it is her son's home, nevertheless regrets the failure in hospitality (S 56).

The audience would be aware of Nanna's position; many would remember the folk belief that all travelers should be received with kindness, as if one were welcoming Christ or a saint. They would share, too, the settled population's distrust of the tinkers because of their unorthodox life-style and their reputation for dishonesty. The play *Sive* accents the peasants' fear of the tinker's curse. Here folk belief in the power of language is also related to the satires of the traveling poets. It has been said of the blind poet Raftery and others that when they were offended, they delivered the most scathing verses against their opponents, and Synge records that among the country people of Wicklow "the tramps, and tinkers who wander round from the west have a curious reputation for witchery and unnatural powers."[8] The tinkers add this mystical dimension to *Sive*. At the same time, their incantations only heighten the emotion; they have no power to change the direction of the action.

The spell-binding effect of the song and the look of the tinkers declaiming it is particularly powerful in performance. It gives an aura of primitive ritual to the play. In the program notes to the 1985 Abbey production, Fintan O'Toole observes that the songs of the tinkers are as essential to the structure of *Sive* as the chorus in a Greek play. He contends that Sive's ordeal has the direct emotional impact of a folksong because of the recurrent musical motif and the presence of the tinkers "as attendant spirits to curse and bless and finally to lament."[9] Such characters are larger-than-life, but their appropriateness to a play set in modern Kerry, however puzzling to an American reader, has already been established. Even without assurance of their authenticity, the outsiders in Keane's early plays function as elements of place. They remind the audience that one's heritage is a gauge by which contemporary Ireland measures events. It is this sense of the past that *Sive* shares with the peasant tradition in the Irish theater; however, the spirit of place pervades the play in order to comment on contemporary social structures. Pats Bocock and Carthalawn not only evoke the cultural landscape of Kerry but also function as commentators on the action, as when, in the guise of giving news, they comment on Sive's impending wedding:

> On the road from Abbeyfeale,
> Sure I met a man with meal,
> Come here, said he, and pass your idle time;
> On me he made quite bold
> Saying the young will wed the old
> And the old man have the money for the child.

> (S 55)

Through their indirect way of letting Mena and the others know that the "secret" arrangements with Sean Dota are already the talk of the village, they allow the audience to catch a glimpse of the world beyond the cottage. Without the steadying influence of ordinary life, the ordeal of Sive could assume cosmic proportions. The play, however, is not a tragedy. The matchmaker and the tinkers keep the nature of Sive's conflict within the perspective of human, not divine, experience. While Carthalawn supplies the imprecations of doom, his father issues social commentary in prose. On their first appearance, Pats speaks of the word going around the village of Sive's impending marriage to an old man; his words are brief and subject to a range of interpretations (S 55–56). In the final scene, on the eve of the wedding, his tone becomes prophetic, and there is no mistaking his opinion as he assesses the signs of the times:

> There is money making everywhere. The fact of the country is changing. The small man with the one cow and the pig and the bit of bog is coming into his own. He is pulling himself up out of the mud and the dirt of the years. He is coming away from the dunghill and the smoky corner. The shopkeeper is losing his stiffness. 'Tis only what I see in my travels. The farmer will be the new lord of the land. What way will he rule? What way will he hould [sic] up under the new money? There will be greater changes everywhere. The servant boy is wearing the collar and tie. The servant girl is painting and powdering and putting silkified stockings on her feet and wearing frilly small clothes under her dress. 'Tis only what I see in my travels. The servant will kick off the traces and take to the high road. Money will be in a-plenty. (He points at Sean Dota.) The likes of him will be the new lords of the land. God help the land! (S 104)

Thus, the tinkers are both features of the landscape and also critical observers.

Keane's handling of the outsiders in Sive is a prototype for his treatment of similar characters in his later plays. In every instance the outsider disrupts the confined world of the cottage and acts as the inciting force of the drama. Such characters can be tramps, poets, or returning emigrants; what they share is the capacity of changing, at least for a time, the lives of the settled community. In her study of the peasant drama, Brenna Katz Clarke refers to the frequency with which outsiders occur in the plays as a means of disturbing peasant lives and attitudes.[10] She cites Yeats's "Pot of Broth" and Synge's "In the Shadow of the Glen" as well as the characters of Christy in The Playboy of the Western World and the old woman in "Cathleen ni Houlihan." In each play, the entrance of the stranger disturbs the status quo and challenges the expectations of the peasantry.

The arrival of the outsider is a standard device in world drama. It becomes a particularly Irish phenomenon because of a twofold frame of reference. First, the stranger, especially since the seventeenth century, has been a figure of the English presence in Ireland, and second, because of this association, the stranger represents any invader. For years after the establishment of the Irish Free State, Ireland followed an isolationist policy which severely limited its political, economic, and intellectual exchange with other countries. Therefore, the stranger in Irish literature represents the intrusion of any outside influence that might result in a change in Irish mores. Clarke concludes that, while the function of the intruding character varies from play to play, the outsider brings with him a feeling of the larger world which broadens, and perhaps threatens, the peasants' life-style. She finds that "there is a suggestion that the playwrights saw the peasant as repeatedly disturbed by outside forces and that, in some cases, it was desirable to shake up the peasant life which tends to be fixed and conservative."[11] This concept of an outsider's impact on the rural scene actually defines the place rather than the character. The closed society is typical of the rural Southwest; it represents, by extension, the insularity of Ireland attempting to deal with its national identity in the face of a rapidly changing modern world.

John B. Keane's early plays clearly follow the pattern of the peasant play, and it seems likely that the catalytic function of the outsider becomes even more relevant when his later plays are read as social commentary. In Sharon's Grave the stranger is a wandering thatcher, Peadar Minogue. His arrival at the Conlee cottage coincides with the old man's death, but the change he brings is quite different from the matchmaker's in Sive. Peadar provides a chance for peace in a divided family and the hope of a solution to their problems. In addition, he participates in the unique history of the wanderer in Irish life and literature.

The wandering figure seems always to have been a part of the cultural landscape of Ireland; his history has been marked by varying attitudes within conventional society. Maureen Waters, in her study The Comic Irishman, suggests that stories of wanderers probably begin with the mobility of the ancient Irish who were accustomed to move with their livestock to seasonal pastures. With the advent of English rule, the government became fearful of the Irish rovers and attempted to exercise some control over them. The tinkers and travelers of modern times seem to have developed from the dispossessed landowners of the eighteenth century and the famine and evictions of the nineteenth century.[12] At first, the settled peasantry treated the travelers with kindness; later, as emigration became the outlet for the landless Irish, tramps became fewer and distrust of the travelers increased among farmers and townspeople. Waters finds that "Associated with the tinkers, who were regarded as promiscuous thieves, they had become outsiders, threatening to the small farmers and the slowly emerging middle class. So the tramp becomes an appropriate symbol for Synge and Beckett, artists who set themselves in opposition to conventional society."[13] Synge elaborates on the artistic interpretation of the wanderer. He states that the poorest member of the family, usually a writer or artist, often sinks to becoming a tramp.[14] From the premise that the artistic individual lacks business sense, Synge draws the analogy of the artist as outsider, and there are also other instances in which the travelers are assigned symbolic meanings. Bothroyd notes that Yeats associates them with the wandering Jew and that Lady Gregory alludes to the folk belief that the wanderer is Christ or a saint in her play *The Travelling Man*.[15] Stage use of the wandering figure often combines the Irish phenomenon with stock roles from theater history. Thus the traveler may share some of the characteristics of the "rogue" or Stage Irishman. Whatever his characteristics, the traveling figure is a commonplace in Irish peasant drama, and Keane's characters share the theatrical heritage of Boucicault and Synge.

It has been suggested that the thatcher in *Sharon's Grave* is a deliverer; he participates in the cult of the lost leader who returns at the moment of crisis and effects release for his people. As wanderer, Peadar Minogue is less significant than Hiker Lacey because it is his interaction with the Conlee family which is important, not his traveling. Keane's *The Year of the Hiker* specifically contrasts the wandering figure with conventional family life and brings forward the folk beliefs and prejudices associated with a man of the road.

The Year of the Hiker, although set in a period almost contemporaneous with *Sive*, seems to be a more modern play probably because there are fewer folk references. Hiker Lacey, however, does share the heritage of the outsider in life and literature. He is branded as irresponsible and dangerous. Unlike other outsiders, such as the matchmaker or the thatcher or the healer Pats Bo Bwee, Hiker Lacey does not follow an occupation which requires him to travel; he has simply left his home and family for life on the road. In this respect, he could be interpreted as a symbol of revolt against authority and conventional society which marks the rogue-heroes of the Boucicault melodramas and Joyce's Stephen Dedalus. What separates Hiker Lacey from the traditional wandering figures is his personal suffering and the conditions that forced him to choose escape. He is a commentary on conventional family life rather than a stereotype.

The Hiker's entrance is carefully anticipated and certainly controls the development of the action, for nothing is ever the same again; however, the returning father's impact differs from the expectations raised by the first scene. The action unfolds in the kitchen of the farmhouse on a day of great excitement, the wedding of the daughter of the house. The surface activity seems normal until the audience realizes the repetition of the motif of the missing father. Oddly, it is not his wife or children who initiate the recollection, but Freda, Kate Lacey's sister. She comments that Simey is much like his father (Hiker 12), and she challenges her sister to recall the years of her marriage and to think about his absence on such an important day. As each character passes through the kitchen, Freda keeps the theme of the father alive until the exposition has been completed, and the audience is ready to receive the irresponsible Hiker Lacey. Freda's voice is a strident chorus, urging each of the others to express the personal pain resulting from the Hiker's long separation from his family. Her own memories are mute except for her humming "Red Sails in the Sunset," and she insists that her role has been to keep the family together. There is a great deal of hateful language directed at the absent Hiker and a great deal of posturing about what each would do were he to return.

All of this appears to be the ordinary prelude to the return of Hiker Lacey, just as predictable as the entrance of the villain in any melodrama. There is a difference, however, and the clues are Freda's song and her final line as the others go out to the wedding:

> Simey. Well, I have to be off, and listen, Freda, . . . don't look so lonely. Your turn will come too. (*Exits.*)
> Freda. My turn is gone! I lost my place in the line, rearing another woman's family. (Hiker 27)

The audience's expectations that Hiker Lacey will return and interrupt his daughter's wedding are not quite fulfilled. He does return, not for the wedding, but to die. His sickness, as well as the actual sight of the father who was always more legendary than real, alters the sons' responses. As noted above, nothing in the household is ever the same after the arrival of the Hiker. The focus shifts from the complaints of the opening scene to a gradual appreciation of the Hiker's position and a reconciliation.

It is the reversal of the romantic ideal of the wanderer, its reinterpretation in the context of twentieth-century social conditions, that separates this play from the peasant melodramas of the past and situates it among contemporary dramas. It is a similar concern for individual human issues rather than class stereotypes that marks *The Highest House on the Mountain*. The returning son and his new wife set the play in motion, but it is the individual suffering of the characters that is the focus of the play.

Prejudice and distrust of rural folk for city dwellers is an ancient motif; what makes Keane's *The Highest House on the Mountain* particularly Irish is the style of bachelorhood displayed by Mikey and Sonny. Each has chosen an escape from normal sexuality. Mikey, widowed for some years, has reverted to his bachelor state. His craving for food masks his loneliness and his normal sexual appetites:

> Mikey. Imagine a roast goose . . . or chops! There's nothin' in this world or the next as sweet as a chop. Suppose now a fellow came in that door with a fryin' pan full o' chops, I bet you'd Jump up an' eat a few.
> Sonny. I wouldn't care. (HH 4)

In the next breath, Mikey recalls his dead wife and the son whose return they are awaiting. Sonny, in contrast, appears removed from the reality around him; he is overly shy and suffers from a "hurt" that seems to be an obsession rather than a physical disability. The audience eventually learns that his unnatural attitude toward women is the result of an unfortunate misunderstanding.

The devices that mark this play as Irish can be found more readily in the convictions of the characters than in the folk motifs; however, there are some elements of superstition which establish place. The confined world of the play is not only a rural cottage, it is a world inhabited by men without women. In such an enclosure, the entrance of a woman, like the tales of women on sailing ships or in the mines, has an aura of bad luck. Although the play makes no direct reference to this superstition, there is an unsettled atmosphere which seems to combine a fear of change with a deeper spiritual problem. Perhaps the remnants of Irish Jansenism, with exaggerated emphasis on sexual sins, color the tone of the play. These elements are part of the spiritual climate of the west of Ireland; they account for the remoteness of Sonny and his ideal house on the mountain as well as for Mikey's visions of food. They also account for the conservative piety that causes Mikey to freeze out the "sinners" rather than see the human needs of his family.

The stage signals, which identify place in drama, range from the physical setting to the inferences drawn from the characterization. In Keane's plays, the set design provides the initial context and local character types contribute to the audience's appreciation of the sense of place. Whether they are strangers or ordinary villagers, the local characters are important to the theme of an Irish play. They may represent also the angle of social vision that a playwright espouses. In any case, characters in Keane's plays tend to reflect the conditions and attitudes of North Kerry. Combined with other stage signals, they lead to a definition of place that, in turn, provides a clue to meaning.

4

Stage-Use of Language, Music, and Folk Customs

Much of the power of the characterization in Keane's plays results from his command of language and his ability to reproduce the dialect of North Kerry. Like many of his predecessors in the Irish Theatre, Keane's dialogue shares the qualities of imagination and richness that give a lyrical tone to even the most realistic situations. At the same time, the concreteness of the speech recreates local habits of thought. Thus Keane devises vivid portraits that give each scene spontaneity and immediacy. Some commentators find reminiscences of Synge in the eloquence of his folk plays, but Keane claims no such influence. In fact, he finds the folk plays of Fitzmaurice more authentic than those of Synge because Synge's is "not a spoken language" but a dialect developed as an observer among the peasants of Wicklow and Kerry.[1] Keane, like Fitzmaurice, records the language of his native Kerry. Although English has been the dominant language of Kerry for many years, the Kerrymen speak a language strongly influenced by Gaelic vocabulary and sentence patterns. Persons who would never consider themselves Irish-speakers pepper their conversations with Gaelic phrases, and their use of words gives an earthy directness to their discourse.

John B. Keane's own conversation is as vivid as that of any of his creations, and he attributes the qualities of modern Kerry speech to the influences of history and environment. He describes the speech of the region as realistic, an agricultural language, "but as well as being that, it is also a very poetic language." Keane sees himself as part of this poetic tradition, and states that the dialect of North Kerry is unique because it is

the love child of two languages . . . Elizabethan English and Bardic
Irish. Now Bardic Irish is court Irish, distinct from the ordinary
Gaelic universally spoken by the ordinary people of Ireland in the
1600's. Then the Elizabethans came to Ireland and the two languages
fused, particularly in North Kerry where the tradition of Irish speaking is dead for hundreds of years. . . . But these two languages fused,
and gave us a unique means of interpreting the wiles and simplicities
and joys and lunacies and tragedies of my people—of our people
here.[2]

Keane believes that a writer who really knows his own people
and the nuances of his own language and is faithful to these
roots will suceeed. He illustrate this view by recalling the North
Kerry writers and noting that the language used by George Fitzmaurice, Bryan MacMahon, and Maurice Walsh and "by a whole
plethora of good poets, is this practical language which is unique
to us, and we're very proud of it. We're not sure that it's our
entitlement, but we took it nevertheless."[3]

Of the writers he mentioned, Keane is most like Fitzmaurice
in his portrayal of the landscape and people of North Kerry. Both
men write about simple people, the tedium of their daily routine,
and their battles with nature. Arthur McGuiness writes that
George Fitzmaurice presents the Kerry folk "as a stubborn and
insensitive lot who compound the problems in their lives with
petty bickering and unforgiving natures. But as a Kerryman himself, he knows too the lyricism of their dialect and he can reproduce this North Kerry dialect with the accuracy of a native
speaker."[4] The world and language of North Kerry have not
changed much since Fitzmaurice lived there, and these words
could just as readily have been written about John B. Keane.

Keane's grasp of the idiom of Kerry can be demonstrated on
almost any page of his rural plays, and the first indication of his
accuracy can be seen in the number of Irish words or derivations
from Irish words that are scattered throughout the dialogue.
Words like á chroidhe, bocach, gradhbhar, bollav, duchas, gom-
malogue, beán-a-tighe, and tamaill flow as naturally in the conversation as familiar English words. The foreign words do not
impede understanding because they suit both the cadence of the
lines and the characters who are speaking them. The language
gives specificity to the scenes. It is as routine to hear a farmer
speak of a "gabhail of hay" (SG 34) as of "grabbers and snappers"

(SG 39). North Kerry is an agricultural society, and the language contributes to the contours of the landscape.

In addition to the words taken directly from the Gaelic, the plays are filled with Kerry expressions and words made by combining English and Irish forms. The most common practice of joining the two languages consists in adding the Irish suffix "een" to an English word. The diminutive thus formed can be a term of endearment or of ridicule. Another way of combining the languages is by adding "ing" to an Irish verb; thus "ullagoning" can be formed from the Gaelic *ólogon* and is as readily understood in the Kerry countryside as the English word "crying." Jean-Michel Pannecoucke, in speaking of Keane's plays, states: "There are plenty of Gaelic words, of Kerry expressions, each one more colourful than the other, but they are not so literary as to sound unnatural; and it is on hearing one of Keane's plays performed in an Irish theatre that one realizes how close his language is to the one spoken in the world outside."[5] These expressions range from imaginative turns of phrase to sentence patterns modeled on Gaelic originals. These examples from *Many Young Men of Twenty* and *Sharon's Grave* illustrate some characteristics of Kerry speech:

If Miss Seelie saw me now, I was sacked on the spot. (Many 12)

Don't be lonely . . . we'll be home again soon and, sure, won't I be with you the whole time an' won't you be meetin' all the lads over? . . . We'll be home again for a holiday in a year. Sure a year is no length of time, man! (Many 10)

Trying to tell me something? Would you be sick now, by any chance, and not able to dress your thoughts in words? . . . If you're sick, there will be somebody attending to you before we're older. (SG 2)

Grammatical patterns employing the verb "be," where English usage would have used a different form, are typical of the areas of Ireland where English speech retains the flavor of translation from the Gaelic. The phrases "dress your thoughts in words" and "before we're older" have a poetic ring; however, they are representative of the ordinary language of the West of Ireland. It is the highly metaphorical nature of the language that makes it both concretely local and poetic at the same time. In *Sharon's*

Grave, there are passages where the phrases are both lyrical and earthy. One can hear the wind when Trassie describes the "awful screeching like the inside of a pig's bladder if you blew it up and left it off. The goureen roe was calling for the rain in the bog far in—all evening it was on" (SG 64). And Peadar's question about Trassie's kin: "Are they the one drop of blood?" (SG 11) illustrates the concrete and vivid usage of the rural Irishman. Also typical of Keane's area is the use of "so" as in the line "I'll walk a little ways, so" (SG 29). The apparently unneeded word adds the local inflection. These are subtle nuances of language, but the cumulative effect on radio or on the stage is a brilliant reproduction of the North Kerry dialect. It is no small task to recreate the local speech so accurately; however, John B. Keane refuses to consider it a great achievement. He insists that "any fool can write a play if he listens. The world around us, particularly the rural world, is alive with singing language and fabulous characters" (SP 103).

Some of Keane's more memorable characters can be described best by their speech. One does not easily forget the manipulation of the matchmaker in *Sive*:

> Thomasheen Sean Rua never blisters his feet without cause. There is some one who have a great wish for the young lady, this one they call Sive. He have the grass of twenty cows. 'Tis how he have seen her bicycling to the Convent in the village. *(Shakes his head solemnly.)* He is greatly taken by her. He have the mouth half-open when he do be talking about her. 'Tis the *sign* of love, woman! (S 18)

or the spell cast by the tinkers' song:

> May the snails devour his corpse,
> And the rains do harm worse;
> May the devil sweep the hairy creature soon;
> He's as greedy as a sow;
> As the crows behind the plough;
> That black man from the mountain, Seaneen Rua!
>
> (S 53–54)

These figures are part of the Kerry landscape and bring to life the social conditions against which the problems of the Glavin family evolve. The language of the characters both creates the rural backdrop and separates them from it. Instead of merely providing local color, these characters assume independent life as human beings whose actions directly affect the major figures of the plot.

One of the best character delineations through speech occurs in *Many Young Men of Twenty*. Even before he enters, Danger Mullaly, a seller of holy pictures, can be recognized by his song; his appearance and his opening words fulfill our expectations:

> "Oh, rise up, Mikey Houlihan, that brave and dauntless boy. . . ." Mikey Houlihan! Mikey boloney! Shot by accident for Ireland. Twenty-four of his relations drawing state pensions and twenty-four more in government jobs, and here am I, Danger Mullaly, with my box full of holy picture an' short fourpence on the price of a pint. *(Changes tone to intimacy.)* 'Tis frightful quiet, Peg Finnerty, for a mornin' before the train. 'Tis frightful quiet, Tom Hannigan. *(Puts his box on the table.)* That's the lookin' they have at me! You'd swear I was the solicitor that advised Pontius Pilate. . . . *(Changes tone.)* Tom Hannigan, as sure as there's brown bastards in China, I'll pay you the extra fourpence . . . here's a shillin' on the table, a silver shillin', made an' manufactured by tradesmen that had a feelin' for beauty . . . proposed, passed, and seconded herewith . . . one pint of Guinness for a sick man . . . balance to be paid in due course on the word of Danger Mullaly, guilty but insane . . . *(Pause)* . . . Guinness, a porter-maker that had his face on a stamp the same as Parnell. (Many 4)

His remarks are often scattered, intended for no one and for everyone, but when Danger addresses Peg, his language is both pointed and precise, and his idiom has all the verve and color of poetic prose:

> Oh . . . so that's it! . . . because you had a bit o' misfortune, you're goin' to be chantin' like an ordained parish clerk for the rest of your life. *(Loudly.)* You had a baby . . . sure, you're not the first an' you won't be the last. What about it? . . . an' you're grumblin' with a fine bonny boy with limbs as supple as a cat an' a grin on his dial like a drake in the rain. (Many 5)

All of these characters, actually minor figures in their respective plots, are fully fleshed by John B. Keane. He has portrayed them with such particular attention to details of speech, costume, and stage business that they transmit the impact of "place" to the audience. Given the power of Keane's fidelity to the dialect of Kerry, one can appreciate the spellbinding effect of a stage production when the visual arts combine with the verbal to realize the emotional impact of the drama.

All the arts contribute to the ultimate power of a drama, and music as well as speech has particular importance in a Keane play. Perhaps the best example of a recurring musical motif in a realistic play occurs in *Sive* where the travelers Pats Bocock and Carthalawn provide both commentary and an insistent rhythm that paces the progress of the plot. Their presence in the Glavin household at strategic moments in the drama heightens the emotional impact of the story. When the traveling men first appear, their song is the traditional greeting in which the man of the house is honored:

> Oh! Mike Glavin, you're the man;
> You was always in the van;
> With a dacent house to old man and gorsoon;
> May white snuff be at your wake
> Baker's bread and curran-y cake
> And plinty on your table, late and soon.
>
> (S 51–52)

When both Mena and Thomasheen Sean Rua answer their request with ill treatment, the song becomes a curse, sung to the same tune. Their arrival, coinciding with the visit of the matchmaker, provides an opportunity for Thomasheen and Mena to reveal their true characters. It also allows Pats and Carthalawn to display, in the cursing song, the antisocial behavior that creates tension between the travelers and the settled population. At this point in the play, their presence is an expository tool and a device for establishing a sense of place. Their subsequent visits enhance the plot, and the insistent rhythm of the bodhran marks the increasing tension. Their songs comment on the arranged marriage and mock the elderly bridegroom and the greedy Mena and Thomasheen. At the end, their chant is a keen for the drowned Sive:

> Oh, come all good men and true,
> A sad tale I'll tell to you
> All of a maiden fair, who died this day;
> Oh, they drowned lovely Sive,
> She would not be a bride
> And they laid her for to bury in the clay.
> (S 111)

Their commentary and their dirge give Sive the dignity of a tragic heroine, although she was as much a victim as an instrument of her own fate. The musical motif unites the action and underscores the central images of greed for money and land. Among Keane's other plays, only his musicals make such an extended use of songs.

John B. Keane avoids what Robert Hogan calls "the deadening qualities of realism" by employing "the theatrical elements of song, spectacle, color, dance and music."[6] It is clear that *Sive* owes at least part of its emotional force to such devices. The use of a musical motif is more subtle in *The Year of the Hiker;* here, the song "Red Sails in the Sunset" serves as a link with the past and as a symbol of the relationship between Freda and the Hiker. The device appears as a piece of business in the first act when Freda sings the tune as she goes through her daily routine. The song seems to be incidental to the scene and to Freda's character; one's first impression is that any song would do. There is, however, more than a touch of nostalgia about Freda's singing. The refrain of the popular song tells of a lover who "sailed at the dawning" and who will go "sailing no more" once the ship has carried him safely home. The song expresses the longing of a lover for an absent loved one. Attention to the lyrics suggests another level of meaning, and Keane allows the familiar melody to engage the audience gradually by having Freda sing it twice before the encounter between Simey and his father. The Hiker's response to his son reveals the significance of the song, when the old man recalls his life on the road:

> Somebody asked me to sing . . . I was full of cider and the night was gay. I sang a song, but my heart was fit to break after singing it and I never sang it since. I used to sing it for your mother . . . oh, but that was long, long ago when I was a strappin' man with the lungs of a young bull. . . . "Red Sails in the Sunset, Way out on the Sea." (Hiker 52–53)

Finally, the song becomes the symbol of the reconciliation between the Hiker and the women in his home. When they sing together in the final act, the Hiker, Freda, and Kate return to the pleasant memories of their youth. The song is a kind of absolution for all the stored-up misunderstanding; it erases the years of bitterness and pain. Keane does not spare the Hiker from death nor from the cruelty of his sons, but the song-motif tempers his end with a suggestion of restored order.

In addition to the occasional use of musical themes, Keane has written several musicals, notably *The Buds of Ballybunion* and *Many Young Men of Twenty.* As the genre requires, these plays make use of songs and dances in order to advance the action. However, the plays themselves are basically realistic dramas in which the music heightens the emotional impact and relieves the realism with lyricism and humor.

John B. Keane also employs folk customs and traditional activities to express the cultural landscape. Just as familiar figures, such as tinkers and matchmakers, enhance the local setting and stimulate the action, familiar events can serve a similar function. Occasions like patterns, fairs, weddings, and wakes are interruptions of the daily routine that are celebrated in specific ways. The folk customs surrounding each occasion are so well ingrained, and honored to the last detail, that deviations from traditional behavior rarely occur. For the purposes of dramatic action the representation of weddings or wakes provides an activity that the audience can take for granted and against which the real action of the play can proceed. This point can be demonstrated by looking closely at wake scenes in several plays, particularly Keane's *Sharon's Grave,* to observe the manner in which the theatrical devices work together in order to achieve the sense of place.

Wakes in rural Ireland are seldom solemn events, unless the death has been especially tragic, and, in earlier days, the occasion offered one of the few changes in a peasant's routine. William Smyth writes in his recent study of place:

> In rural Ireland, . . . the funeral remains one of the greatest expressions of social life. Funerals are for the living as well as the dead, and the meeting-places of home, church, publichouse and cemetery, associated with the rituals of the dead, bond together communities at specific times. Funerals also reveal all the nuances of kinship-networks, class and status, that Irish society is always so acutely attuned to.[7]

Tradition requires the relatives and neighbors to "wake the corpse"; thus, they visit the house of the deceased during the day and night and receive hospitality in keeping with the financial status of the family. Sean O'Suilleabhain in *Irish Wake Amusements* advances several theories regarding the origin of the custom. He suggests that it is a remnant of the pagan folk ways of dealing with death and the taboos surrounding death.[8] This view would account for the various wake amusements often referred to in Irish fiction as well as in O'Suilleabhain's work. Although superstition is inconsistent with the Christian attitude toward death, the wake is a significant part of the rural scene in Ireland as the last occasion in which the dead and the living share each other's company.[9] Stories recount examples of wild behavior, boisterous games, and tests of dexterity and physical ability, as well as the better known customs of eating, drinking, and story-telling. Estyn Evans agrees that, while evidence cannot support a coherent pattern among the Irish peasants, "it is clear that the cathartic extravagance of the wakes not only served to dissipate over-charged tensions but were closely concerned with ancestral spirits and perpetuation of the life of the community."[10]

Whatever the games were in the various regions, the social aspects of the wake remained constant throughout Ireland. The well-established customs of keening and story-telling, in addition to the provisions of food, drink, and tobacco, continue to the present. The body of the deceased is now removed from the home to the Church on the evening before the burial.[11] Father Anthony Gaughan, in his history of Listowel, comments only briefly on wake customs:

> In the houses of comfortable farmers, the men were treated to drink, tobacco, clay-pipes and snuff in the kitchen and the ladies were taken into "the room" for tea and gossip . . . there is no evidence that North Kerry wakes were ever other than decorous and solemn, with story-telling as the only form of entertainment.[12]

His description portrays the traditional wake, and he notes that some of the customs have declined in recent years. The old ways fade slowly in the west of Ireland, and it is the older customs that survive in representations of wakes in the theater.

Before discussing the wake scene in *Sharon's Grave* and its relation to this consideration of sense of place, a brief examination of two familiar wake scenes in earlier plays, namely Boucicault's *The Shaughraun* and Synge's "In the Shadow of the Glen," is necessary. These plays are similar to Keane's in that

they use the folk customs concerning death as a frame for the
larger issues of the play. They differ from *Sharon's Grave* because
their "corpses" are only feigning death.

Stories of individuals who pretend to die in order to achieve
a particular goal are common in folklore and literature. Synge's
play adds a reversal to the plot and leaves the husband with the
woman's lover, while she takes to the road with the tramp. In
this study the details of the "wake" are more relevant than the
turn of the plot. The stage directions describe the scene:

> Cottage kitchen; turf fire on the right; a bed near it against the wall,
> with a body lying on it covered with a sheet. A door is at the other
> end of the room, with a low table near it, and stools, or wooden
> chairs. There are a couple of glasses on the table, and a bottle of
> whiskey, as if for a wake, with two cups, a tea-pot, and a home-made
> cake. There is another small door near the bed. Nora Burke is moving
> about the room, settling a few things, and lighting candles on the
> table, looking now and then at the bed with an uneasy look.[13]

Ordinarily, the body of the deceased would have been dressed
in its shroud by some women, not members of the family, who
had particular skill at the task. In this play, the remoteness of the
cottage and the curse that Nora fears account for the corpse's
not being appropriately laid out. These conditions also explain
Burke's success at pretending death. Synge's scene in the mountain cabin, while it will differ from the other two plays, accurately depicts the custom. In fact, Nora's apology to the Tramp
because she can only offer him one of her husband's pipes recalls
the custom of providing new clay pipes, already filled with tobacco, for all the visitors. Even the omission adds authenticity to
the scene. The poverty of the house and the dearth of visitors
underscore very effectively the isolation of the cottage. Although
the husband wishes to trick her into exposing her infidelity, the
play becomes a story of Nora's loveless marriage and of the influence of place in the lonely districts in the west of Ireland.

The Boucicault play employs the feigned death for an entirely
different purpose and in a totally different tone. Conn, *The
Shaughraun*, is a rogue-hero, and he is at the center of a melodrama involving landlords and their agents, wronged heroines,
and young heroes at odds with the English law. It is less important for us to outline the progress of the plot than to notice

Boucicault's use of the wake traditions in order to unravel the complications. The scene of Conn's wake is set in his mother's cabin, and the stage directions supply the traditional picture of an Irish wake:

> Conn is lying on a shutter, supported by an old table, a three-legged stool, and a keg. Table covered with food and drinking cups, plates of snuff, jugs of punch. . . . Tableau of an Irish Wake. A group of women around Conn, Mrs. O'Kelly seated; Mrs. Malone and Reilly near her. Sullivan, Doyle, and peasantry (male and female) at table. The women are rocking to and fro during the wail.[14]

The scene continues while the traditional keening of the women recalls the virtues of the deceased, and their frequent sips of punch portray the Stage Irish stereotypes. Both the praise and the drink are too much for Conn to resist, and the "corpse" reveals to the audience that he is very much alive. This broad humor is quite different from Synge's use of the same device. The humorous tone portends the happy ending; the information regarding the villain's hide-out is overheard by the corpse; the heroine is rescued and the appropriate characters punished.

The Shaughraun and "In the Shadow of the Glen" employ customary attitudes and actions to further the purposes of the action. Synge's realistic approach subordinates the device to his theme, while Boucicault draws on all the stereotypes of wake behavior in order to entertain as well as to contrive a solution to the problems of the play. Both plays evoke a sense of the Irish countryside in their use of familiar customs as a backdrop to the central action.

John B. Keane's use of a wake is closer to Synge than to Boucicault. Although touched by grotesque elements, Sharon's Grave is fundamentally a realistic play. The dual strains of local custom and Catholic practice form a frame for the action, and, while the death of the elder Conlee is central to the narrative, the prescribed customs of the wake are so well-known that they function in the same way as painted scenery. The stage directions reproduce the scene of any Irish wake:

> The room is changed inasmuch as there are now several plush-covered chairs in it. On the bed the old man lies dead. He is facing the audience slightly propped up. He is dressed in a frilly brown ha-

bit. . . . Six assorted brass candlesticks, holding lighted candles
stand on a table. There is also a saucer filled with snuff on the
table. . . . A rosary beads is entwined in his hands. (SG 24)

Together the visual and verbal elements present the North Kerry
locale in which the struggle for the Conlee house continues. The
scene opens with visitors to the house greeting Neelus and then
advancing to the bed:

Moll. Ah! God bless him, isn't he a handsome corpse!
Mague. He's lovely, the fine dacent man.
Moll. That had a hard word for no one.
Mague. That would give you the bite he'd be eatin'.
.   .   .   .
Moll. (to Neelus) Where's Trassie?
Neelus. She's feeding the visitors in the kitchen.
Moll. Is there many of them there?
Mague. Did your cousins from Luascawn come?
Moll. What about your mother's people from Lenamore? (SG 25)

These women, although unimportant to the plot, are essential
to the authenticity of this scene. Any gathering in a rural community will bring together persons who have little access to news
at other times. Moll and Mague represent those members of society who sit at a wake and carefully observe the rest of the townspeople as they pass before them. John B. Keane explains that the
wake scene was based on his own experience. He tells of being
under close scrutiny by the women of the town

who would have no other way of examining me at close quarters
than having me kneeling. They could count the number of hairs on
my head. They can as well see if women, they're wearing wigs. . . .
They can see all these things because here they have . . . a well-lit
scene, absolute silence, where they can fold their hands and examine
her from head to toe. . . . This is the only opportunity they've got
of knowing anything—especially people who live in very isolated
areas. . . . the wake room was an academy, it was a mine, a source of
information; it was a library of local defects and blemishes.[15]

Keane manages to convey to the stage the North Kerry wake
as he has experienced it. His skill not only recreates a specific
custom but also brings to life the community in which the Conlee family resides. One can observe the questions Moll and
Mague put to Neelus, and later to Trassie, their looks and whis-

pers in the direction of the stranger, and their comments on the other visitors.

These two women are the centerpiece of the wake scene, but the old man, the schoolteacher, and the other mourners also give a cross-section of the rural settlement. The old man, Tom Shawn, offers a vital insight into the peasant mind, particularly in Ireland, as he attempts to identify the family background of the thatcher. Since Peadar is a stranger, his ancestry and connections are topics of curiosity, and the preoccupation with one's lineage is a typically Irish trait. Tom Shawn makes several unsuccessful tries at naming the branch of the Minogues to which Peadar belongs; finally, he succeeds in making a connection:

> *Tom Shawn.* (brightly) What would your mother's name be now? Is she alive or dead?
> *Peadar.* She's dead this long time, the Lord ha' mercy on her. From Errimore, a Hennessy.
> *Tom Shawn.* (reflectively) Hennessys from Errimore, Hennessys from Errimore. Hennessys. There was a Timmineen Hennessy, a flamin' stepdancer, from the Errimore side. Would they be the one Hennessys?
> *Peadar.* Timmineen Hennessy was my granduncle.
> *Tom Shawn.* Glory be to us all, but isn't it a small world? . . . And you tell me Timmineen Hennessy was your granduncle? Sure his feet were like forks of lightning. He would dance on a threepenny bit for you.
>
> . . . .
>
> and Timmineen Hennessy to be your granduncle. Was there ever better than that. (SG 28)

The tone of the scene shifts slightly when the schoolteacher enters; it is evident that she is of a higher social class than the others present. Throughout this portion of the play, Trassie circulates among the visitors either inviting them to the kitchen for food or offering them drinks. It is a faithful reproduction of an ordinary wake in a small community, until the arrival of Jack and Dinzie alters the focus of the scene.

Dinzie Conlee is maimed in mind as well as in body, and we have drawn comparisons between his crippled appearance and the starkness of the landscape. In this scene, his actions border on the wild games alluded to in the studies of folk customs and wakes; however, Dinzie deliberately flouts the social conventions represented by the seated mourners:

Dinzie. (to corpse) Are you dead, Donal? Are you dead, I say? Look at the face of him, Jack. Are you dead, Donal, I say? Will you have me talking to myself? Is he dead, Jack?

Jack. (placatingly), wisha, Dinzie, he's dead all right. Leave him alone and don't be tormenting him.

.   .   .   .

Dinzie. (to Moll and Mague) What business have ye here? A nice pair of oul' hags, snuffin' an' gossipin' an' drinkin' your little sups of wine an' cuttin' an' backbitin' everybody. *(Jack carries him to where Miss Dee sits)*

Dinzie. Who left you in?

Miss Dee. I came to pay respect to the dead.

Dinzie. You came spyin' to see who was here. Why don't you get an oul' man for yourself an' get married.

.   .   .   .

Miss Dee. You should be on your knees praying for your dead uncle.

Dinzie. Should I now?

Miss Dee. Yes, you should, and show a little respect for the dead.

Dinzie. Give her a lick of the fist, Jack. Go on, Jack!

Jack. Ah, can't you go aisy, Dinzie! Isn't it in a wake room we're in?
(SG 31–32)

Dinzie's chief interest in this scene, as in the earlier action, is in owning his uncle's house; therefore, he continues to pursue Trassie with his demand that she turn the house over to him. Trassie ignores him. Her refusal, plus his drinking, sets Dinzie on a tirade. He effectively disrupts the wake and clears the room of visitors. The scene ends, finally, as Dinzie leaves to design a new plan of action.

A stage production of *Sharon's Grave* would surely concentrate on the pairs of cousins: Trassie and Neelus and Jack and Dinzie. Their relationships with each other and to the landscape, with its legend of Princess Sharon, are the vital aspects of this play. It would, however, be a serious error to ignore the minor characters, particularly the characters in the wake scene. The rural setting, especially an isolated farm cottage, does not allow for the interaction of many characters. Consequently, Keane intends the wake to be important to a realization of the local community. The vigor of the superstition that remains just below the surface of everyday life is so carefully portrayed that it would be difficult to separate the characters from the landscape.

Barry Cassin, a director who has often worked with Keane contends that an urban audience might miss the importance of the minor characters and the gathering in the house of the deceased. In an interview with this writer, he recalled a production of *Sharon's Grave* in which some characters had been cut, thereby drastically changing the mood of the wake scene. He believes that the director's decision indicated a flagrant misreading of the play because it divorced the story of the Conlees from the environment which created the situation. Both Cassin and James N. Healy, who created the role Pats Bo Bwee in the original production, agree that the characters create the neighborhood. They are convinced that the folk plays of Keane lose something of their power unless the director is well acquainted with the traditions of rural Ireland.[16]

This incident suggests that a misinterpretation of the local scene could change the nature of a Keane play. *Sharon's Grave*, in particular, could become a fantasy if the grotesque characterizations were not consistently tempered by a realistic treatment of the setting and the local characters. An appreciation of Keane's use of place, then, is necessary for an understanding of the various kinds of behavior in the play. The characters emerge from the landscape; the cultural and spiritual milieu has shaped their attitudes and their experience. To miss the importance of place is to misread the play.

It is a serious error to approach even a modern Irish play with notions of life and human relationships drawn from television or urban experience. A careful reader of John B. Keane's works will be mindful that he depicts characters and situations from rural Ireland, and the effort will yield both a deeper appreciation of the nuances of humor in the plays and a grasp of the social implications. Keane is, after all, a modern writer, and, by his careful attention to the details of Irish life, he intends not only to entertain but also to explore the tensions between tradition and contemporary social conditions in the lives of individuals.

5

Contexts for Social Criticism

Just as local characters and customs make up the cultural land-scape of Ireland, certain values and attitudes also contribute to the spiritual milieu known as the spirit of place. Literary representations of these values result in a recurrence of certain themes in the history of Irish literature. These familiar motifs, along with the descriptions of specific locales and characters, express the sense of place in contemporary Irish drama. Among the themes, listed by Daniel Corkery as land, religion, and politics, is a consistently repeated quest for personal and national identity. Therefore, a study of place must take into account the subjects that have concerned Irish writers through the years. Current social and economic topics have supplanted political self-determination as motifs for drama; however, the basic categories remain. The difference, as Robert Hogan suggests in his introduction to *Seven Irish Plays,* is that the thrust of contemporary plays is more often toward the individual than the national: "The themes of the older Irish plays were usually, in a descending scale of importance, either for or against money, land, the made marriage, patriotism and hero worship, social climbing, emigration, and the clergy. We still find these themes, but we find them translated into terms of individual anguish rather than seen as uniquely national problems."[1] Hogan contends that the trend toward individualism produces plays with a more universal appeal. The fact remains that Irish plays, and Keane's in particular, are very often more regional than universal. It is the shift toward social commentary that links his plays with the mainstream of modern drama. Keane's use of the traditional themes does not mark a return to the peasant plays of the Celtic Revival; rather, his practice breaks with an Abbey tradition that outlawed social criticism. Simultaneously, the time-honored themes contribute to the sense of place. Both the setting and the motifs provide a context for the playwright's exploration of individual problems and for his reflections on Ireland's position in the modern world. Economic concerns take a variety of forms, but, in the folk plays, the traditional associations of land and dowry with marriage and emigration are most important. Contemporary Ireland is several generations removed from the Land Acts of 1903, and the subject of land ownership does not dominate the stage as in the first days of the Irish National Theatre. But Padraic Colum's *The Land* does have successors in Keane's early work, *The Highest House on the Mountain* and *Sharon's Grave*, when he describes both the obsession with passing the farm to one's sons and the status conferred on individuals who own property. His later plays, *The Field* and *Big Maggie*, heighten this concern by demonstrating the violence which can accompany the lust for money and land. In *the Highest House on the Mountain* Keane presents the economic issues rather obliquely: he suggests that the problems of life in rural Ireland today are caused, in part, by the conditions which make it necessary for the young to leave the farms in order to find work. Other Keane plays, notably *Hut 42*, tackle the relationship of economics and emigration more directly. In *Sharon's Grave*, preoccupations with status and sex are mixed with Dinzie Conlee's desire for land, and some plays, such as *The Chastitute*, explore the themes of frustration and loneliness. These plays of Keane suggest that the concern for land is emblematic of other realities in modern life; namely, the economic pressures in Ireland and the frustrations resulting from an unnatural obsession with sex.

Important to the theme of land is the Irish concern for name and family, and this leads to a consideration of the problem of authority. From the early days of pagan Ireland, a king's rule over a particular region was ratified by a ritual symbolizing his marriage with the land, the Sovereignty of Ireland which was personified as a woman. Through the years female deities, warriors, and personifications of the land have dominated Irish history and literature. These figures represent both the womanhood of Ireland and the land itself. From the ancient ritual of coronation, through layers of oral and written history, the strong woman survives as an avatar of Ireland and appears in drama as Maura in "Riders to the Sea" and as O'Casey's Juno Boyle. In modern

drama, the unequivocal symbol of the Sovereignty of Erin becomes an individual struggling with a variety of problems in a
context of hereditary mores and values. Keane's focus on women
seems to indicate both his continuation of the dominant female
personification in Irish Literature and his realization that this
persona must represent individuals within a regional frame instead of national stereotypes. The antique association of the
woman and the land undoubtedly contributes to the competition
for supremacy when two women occupy the same house. There
can be both real and figurative problems of authority, and Keane's
plays *Sive* and *The Year of the Hiker* offer two views of this
phenomenon.

In *Sive*, there is the typical disagreement of mother-in-law and
daughter-in-law. Their relationship is marked by resentment and
Mena's assertion of her position: "I have every right to this house.
I paid dear for my share" (S 15). Nanna responds by referring to
Mena's background: "You should have stayed in your father's
house. . . . Your father *(derisively)* a half-starved bocock of a beg-
gar with the Spanish blood galloping through his veins like lit-
ters of hungry greyhounds" (S 16). Even after years of marriage,
Mena is insecure in her own home, and her childlessness heightens her resentment of Sive, the illegitimate child of Nanna's
daughter. Mena's eagerness for Sive's marriage stems both from
financial need and her desire for undisputed authority in the
cottage. Her advice to Sive is a reflection of her own experience:

> All I know is that you will be independent. I know that you will
> never want for a shilling and that you will never have the fear of the
> bailiff and you going to your bed at night not knowing but that they
> might be at your door in the morning and the hungry faces and the
> big lorry to steal away your few cows. I know that you will never be
> faced with the shopkeeper when he threatens you with the law be-
> cause you can't pay his bill. You will have no enemy when you have
> the name of money. You will find a friend everywhere. Even the black
> sins on your soul will be laughed away because you are rich.
> (S 66–67)

A first reaction to Mena and Nanna may be to consider only
these material values and dismiss the bickering as a device that
points up Sive's predicament. Naturally, when sympathies are
with Sive, Nanna's side of the argument is also favored. The prob-

lem, however, is deeper and concerns the traditional roles of women in Irish society.

Swayed by its sympathy for Nanna and Sive, the audience may fail to understand that Mena, as wife of the man of the house, should exercise authority at the hearth. Conrad Arensberg in *The Irish Countryman* speaks at length on the changing relationships within the family when a son marries. The marriage contract includes the payment of the dowry to the father of the groom who, in turn, signs over the land to his son. The old couple continue to live on the farm although they relinquish active control. This stepping aside in favor of the younger couple reserves to the older couple the best room in the house, the west room, and certain other marks of respect, in addition to their maintenance.[2] The relationship between Nanna and Mena is difficult to reconcile with this custom; Nanna consistently subverts Mena's authority, unwilling, it seems, to abdicate her place at the hearth to another woman. According to Arensberg, this kind of problem would ordinarily be settled by deference and respect, but if not, "it is the older woman who must leave . . . the son must cleave to his bride."[3]

It is certainly natural for Nanna to resent a change in the household, and Sive is at the center of the departure from custom. The young girl has been Mike and Nanna's responsibility, and Mena does not share in that special relationship. Having no children of her own, Mena is an unproductive field, a living symbol of the economic hardship of life on the land. In rural Ireland barrenness is considered a curse because it thwarts the "continuity of the husband's line upon the land."[4] Her bargaining with the matchmaker, in this light, becomes less an act of resentment or greed than an attempt to insure her proper place in the household by freeing her of both her female rivals. This analysis of Mena's character does not answer all the questions of her relationship with Nanna and Sive; it only suggests that her antagonism might well be the fruit of frustration and unfulfilled hopes. Nanna is not simply a victim; she must share some blame for the tensions in the cottage. In this light, Mena is the strong, not always lovely, woman of Irish life and literature who supports and sustains the farm and family. She belongs with the women of O'Casey's tenements, and there are at least two sides to her character and her situation.

Both *Sive* and *The Year of the Hiker* present the strength of
the female characters in juxtaposition to the weakness of the
male members of the household. Neither Mike Glavin nor Hiker
Lacey exerts a significant influence in the family except in relation to the women. Although Mena appears to defer to Mike as
head of the house, it is clear that she actually makes the major
decisions. He protests against Sive's marriage at first; then he
agrees to it, probably to keep the peace. His only assertion of his
proper role comes in this exchange with his mother:

> I was a dutiful son to you, but a man marries and his world will
> change to suit his marriage. There is only room for two, mother, only
> for two and if someone new comes into it, a one that's inside must
> go out . . . before I took a wife I was a good son. After I took a wife
> I changed from a son to a husband. Surely you will not blame me
> for that. (S 84)

Although Hiker Lacey dominates the action of *The Year of the
Hiker*, it is Freda who controls the initial perception of his character. It is she who sets up the exposition of the narrative and
reminds the audience, by condemning him openly and often, of
the Hiker's negligence and her own sacrifices for the family. Mike
Glavin and Hiker Lacey are part of the long line of failed fathers
in Irish literature. They, like Simon Dedalus, are examples of
ineffectual leaders, who recall similar lost leaders in the religious and political arenas.

Keane's appreciation of the failed-father image and the strong
female influence in Irish life differs somewhat from that of James
Joyce. Joyce's hero Stephen Dedalus is haunted throughout his
adventures by the memory of his mother, while, at the same time,
he rebels against the fathers, the figures of authority in his life.
In the plays under discussion, however, the dominant female
figures are not mothers. Mena Glavin is childless and frustrated
by her state; the nurturing of Sive is left to her grandmother. In
The Year of the Hiker, the strong character is Freda, the unmar-
ried sister of Kate Lacey. The Hiker's wife appears to be a gentle,
somewhat weak individual, while her sister exerts the leadership
one would expect from the head of a household. Unlike Joyce,
who assigns to his female characters, and thereby, to Mother
Ireland and Mother Church, the attributes of both nurturing and

stifling love from which Stephen must escape, Keane presents Mena and Freda as characters who experience motherhood vicariously by rearing another woman's children. Another author might give symbolic overtones to such a relationship; Keane, however, does not invite a reading of his works as commentary on national politics. His shift of focus, from traditional images of motherhood, suggests, rather, that one examine the individual and her personal suffering within a local community. Keane asks the audience to find a message in his plays only to the extent that an individual's pain can be emblematic of existing social conditions.

The Year of the Hiker also presents the Freda-Kate relationship as another example of the struggle for authority in the household. The antagonisms in Sive correspond, at least on the surface, to mother-in-law and daughter-in-law stereotypes. In contrast, the sisters in The Year of the Hiker give every indication of mutual support and love; although Freda has usurped the authority of the hearth, Kate seems willing to occupy the secondary position. The clues to their relationship can be found in the opening scene where Freda's role in the conversation about the missing father has already been cited. The same dialogue and the accompanying action show that it is Freda who cautions Simey on his drinking, organizes the daily routine, and adds the motherly touches of adjusting the boys' ties. She is the one who remains away from the wedding because she has taken on herself the responsibility of the house and farm. Her sister's children honor Freda and consult her on the ordinary concerns of their lives. She dominates the stage in the opening scene, and Kate Lacey's brief appearance underscores Freda's position of authority in the household.

The opening scene sets up the family relationships by inference. The audience learns the importance of specific characters by interpreting the signals of time and space allotted to each. It is appropriate, then, that Freda is alone in the house when the Hiker returns, just as it is fitting that she hums "Red Sails in the Sunset" while she performs her routine tasks. The Hiker's arrival and the exchange of accusations between him and Freda make it clear that there is another side to his wandering than the one already presented:

Hiker. I came back . . . 'twas the year after I left. I stood outside there
and looked in and the heart was torn out of me. You were here in
the kitchen with her . . . with Kate. . . . Ye looked happy enough
. . . only that I should be sittin' where you were sittin'. 'Twas me
or you, Freda. You were husband, father, mother and aunt, all rolled
up in one. I came away from the window that night and I asked
myself—has no one pity for those who think different, for those
that can't rest. You didn't want me. Ye had my children and that
was enough for ye.

Freda. Yes . . . you had your freedom and your wife had a broken
heart.

Hiker. She broke her own heart. Kate was a mouse, but I loved her. I
couldn't make her into a woman with you around. We could do
nothing with you. There was no peace or fulfillment in our love-
making with you in the house. Even in our privacy there was your
shadow hanging over us.

Freda. I never said a word against you!

Hiker. And you never said a word for me! You never tolerated me
because you couldn't boss me, but you got between us. (Hiker 31–
32)

This exchange disposes the audience to accept the Hiker with
more sympathy than his family expresses, and subtle changes
begin to occur in the household. Joe and Simey remark that Freda
has been different since their father's return (Hiker 38). Joe
gradually assumes greater authority; he becomes the head of the
household as Freda's influence wanes. Other significant changes
occur in the attitudes of Simey and Joe. The older brother grows
in sympathy and attempts to be understanding of his father, but
Simey, said to be like the Hiker in temperament, rejects the old
man. In the course of his taunts, Simey causes his father to reveal
the relevance of Freda's song. Although the young man fails to
grasp the significance himself, the audience recognizes another
dimension of the Hiker's relationship with Freda. The whole
truth surfaces in the play, first as bitterness:

Hiker. I never learned but one thing, and it's too late now to benefit
from it. I learned that the shelter of a bush with two people is
better than a palace with three. (Hiker 77)

As the accusations flow from both Freda and Hiker, it becomes
clear that Freda felt betrayed by her sister's marriage (Hiker 79);
she had believed that the Hiker favored her. Finally, he is able to

make her see that her interference was really the cause of his leaving, and the realization stuns her with remorse:

> Hiker. Can you think of another reason, of a better reason? You wouldn't let our marriage alone. You never accepted it. . . . I had my dignity as a man. . . . I'd be ashamed to tell my friends that there were two women in my house who wouldn't play their parts. . . . I'd be shamed to say that the women of my house were breaking me between them . . . were breaking my pride and spirit because neither was woman enough to face up to the truth.
> Freda. Oh, what a terrible mess we made of it all! O Merciful Holy Mother, forgive me! (Hiker 79–80)

The reconciliation of the Hiker with Freda and Kate comes as they reminisce about their youth. The song which unites their experience has been the cover for Freda's frustration just as surely as the Hiker's rebellion has been his only way of coping with two women competing for authority in the home. The scenes that bring together the Hiker's impulse toward wandering and Freda's assertion of control in the family, as well as the other characters' varying needs, make ordinary events seem larger than life. It is likely that John B. Keane intends to portray the level of frustration and unfulfilled dreams in the individual lives. In any case, the motifs of two women at the same hearth, the traveler and the failed-father illustrate the Irish preoccupation with land and authority. These themes provide a regional context for an appreciation of the personal, and thereby universal, suffering of the characters.

These examples demonstrate the specifically Irish concerns for the land and family which emerge as themes in the peasant drama. Clearly associated with the motifs of the land are the political and religious themes that are inseparable from the Irish character. Contemporary plays have less to say about political identity, except for those playwrights who choose to deal with the problems of partition; however, the moral and ethical issues of the plays must be understood in context of religious identity. Part of the unspoken background of The Year of the Hiker and the other plays discussed in this chapter is the influence of religion in the lives of the Irish peasantry. The same people who are devoted to patriotism and political independence have always been bound by faith and rigid tradition to the Catholic Church.

The display of such religious belief on the stage begins with the cottage described in an earlier chapter. Both the playwright and the audience of an Irish kitchen drama would take for granted the holy pictures and the "blessed lamp" which were kept in the kitchen.[5] In addition, the references to "the room" would be understood to mean the west room, used only on the most formal occasions. Among the furnishings of the room were the sacramentals used when the priest came to celebrate Mass or anoint the dying, as well as the special dishes used for the breakfast after the "Station Mass."

These references would be part of the shared experience of an Irish audience. Most spectators would understand that the physical evidence of religion and the allusions to ancient customs point to a system of values that rules life in the present. Arensberg concludes that the value system, entrenched in custom, "dictates attitudes and reflects itself in behavior."[6] This fact can be even more clearly demonstrated when the traditions are part of the Catholic heritage. References to religious practices and moral attitudes permeate the language of the plays. It is commonplace to encounter the name of God and the saints in ordinary dialogue. More formal allusions to Catholic practice can be seen in the stage directions for "grace before meals" (Hiker 62) in *The Year of the Hiker* and the direction that the Hiker enters with beads in his hands (Hiker 64). In addition, inferences based on religious belief are scattered throughout the play and form a frame of reference for the moral stance of the characters:

> *Freda.* They're ashamed of you! The very mention of your name and they start hating you, so for the final time now, come on. Do this one good thing in your life and maybe God will have mercy on you for the wrong things you've done.
> *Hiker.* Let me alone! Your God and my God are different people. I came too far to go away again. (Hiker 33)

Both here and in Simey's reaction to his father, God's mercy is defined in relation to selfish concerns. Freda's God is one who recognizes only the conservative behavior of the settled "good" people; the Hiker, instead, has learned in his travels that the good, respectable people of this world can be very cruel to those who differ from the social norm. The entire play has the ring of the return of the Prodigal Son, and the varying reactions from those at home, whose complacency has been disturbed, illustrate several interpretations of the Christian idea of forgiveness. The shared experience of Irish Catholicism and its often rigid moral stance forms a background against which the contemporary scene is played.

In *The Highest House on the Mountain*, Mikey illustrates moral rigidity in his attitude toward his daughter-in-law, who he learns had been a prostitute (HH 61). His first response is the Jansenistic stereotype one would expect, with righteous indignation condemning sexual license. The audience eventually learns that he drives her out of his house, not because of her sin, but because "I couldn't dare trust myself" (HH 62). This play, like the others, makes its claim for modernity and universality in its portrayal of the frustrations, often due to sexual repression, which characterize the lives of the rural Irish.

Earlier in this study, the grotesque Dinzie Conlee and the relationship of his crippled body to both the wild landscape and his warped mind were noted. The extravagance of this characterization is an indication of some Irish views toward sexuality, and, as such, it illustrates the sense of place. In *Sharon's Grave*, both Dinzie and Neelus, his cousin, are obsessed with the idea of sex, and both border on madness. Neelus spends his time peering into a deep hole near the cliffs, which is associated with a beautiful princess, Sharon, and her ugly maid Shiofra. The parallel between the pair of cousins and the ill-fated Sharon and Shiofra becomes increasingly apparent as the drama progresses. The figures from legend embody both the beauty of sex and the ugliness that destroys the beauty. The simple Neelus, in order to save the farm for his sister, reverses the legend, carries the evil Dinzie to Sharon's Grave, and plunges into the hole with him. The energy in the play results from combining the folk mysteries associated with the landscape with a violent confrontation between healthy and unhealthy sexuality.

Besides this use of folk legend and grotesque characters, Keane's attempts to illustrate the daily struggles of individuals have resulted in a cast of sympathetically drawn women characters. Phyllis Ryan notes that even his "anti-heroines, such as Maggie and Mena, are not regarded by audiences as heartless villains. . . . There is a certain sense of identification."[7] Whether he writes about the rural woman or the urban housewife trapped by social conventions, Keane has an unusual insight into the complexities of her situation. He is able to bring to the stage even the psychological stress of Mame Fadden's change of life, and, although the play is not one of his best, Keane presents a woman who is very real. *The Change in Mame Fadden* portrays a woman who is alone within her own family, a woman who has no place. Her inability to resign herself is, as Eileen Moriarty suggests, both her conflict and her tragedy.[8] This story "ends at a bus stop, the very symbol of homelessness. In Ireland, as in America, the bus stop is a term for people in transit; at its worst, it symbolizes the person with no place to go.[9]

Each of his female characters draws on the traditional roles of Irish women, and each demonstrates in some way the failure of the stereotype to portray adequately the genuine concerns and the struggles of individuals within the social system. Keane manages to create both a nostalgia for the vanishing traditions, with their secure social niches, and a sympathy for the men and women trapped by those same traditions.

In most of his plays, Keane illuminates present-day problems against a backdrop of age-old custom. In some cases the folk customs and contemporary values appear to be at war, and the moral dilemmas resulting from the dichotomy between modern life and traditional practice become increasingly evident in his later plays and in his novel *The Bodhran Makers*.

The dramas discussed in this chapter illustrate folk motifs and social conventions at work in contemporary situations. The recurring themes of land, marriage, religion, and authority are part of the cultural landscape of Ireland, and thus are essential to any exploration of place in literature. Keane's early plays, especially when he portrays individual problems rather than national stereotypes, suggest that he is concerned with the struggle between traditional values and the mores of twentieth-century Ireland. His later plays continue to use traditional motifs as commentary. Situating interpretation in the cultural landscape of Ireland, which the stage signals create, brings the audience to a fuller understanding of the social implications of Keane's drama.

6

Lust for Land: *The Field* and *Big Maggie*

The land remains a constant theme. It is part of the heritage, the beautiful and bitter memory of the Irish past. Literature addresses the topic both as a real problem and as a symbolic struggle; consequently, the motifs related to land also represent a search for personal and communal identity. As a theme in Irish dramatic literature, the land is closely associated with name, kinship, the made marriage, and emigration. Because these issues are keyed to the facts of Irish social history, their portrayal in contemporary literature can employ the cultural landscape as a frame for social criticism.

Sense of place in the works of John B. Keane begins with his drawing on the larger-than-life qualities of the Kerry landscape. Any discussion of *The Field* and *Big Maggie*, therefore, must begin with the same premise, particularly because the major character in each drama is a larger-than-life figure. The central characters Bull McCabe and Maggie Polpin embody the problems of their respective plots, and their individual strengths and weaknesses present traits that can be identified with the element of "place" in modern Irish literature.

Bull McCabe dominates the stage and the other characters of *The Field;* he is an ordinary bully and a potential Stage Irishman. It is his singular love for the land that makes him a representative of North Kerry. His desire for the field is reasonable since it borders his own land and provides his only access to water. It is Bull's passion for ownership that sets him apart. McCabe speaks of the care he has lavished on the land, and he considers Mrs. Butler's decision to sell a betrayal of his rights:

> *Bird.* 'Tis a good bit of land though, Bull. You'll have to admit that.
> *Bull.* Oh, I admit it all right but 'twas the manure of my heifers that

made it good. Five years of the best cowdung in Carraigthomond and forty pounds a year for grazing. That's two hundred pounds I paid her, not counting the cost of the cowdung and the thistles we cut year in and year out. To me that field isn't worth a penny over four hundred pounds. Now I've paid her two hundred in rent. I reckon if she got two hundred more from me she'd be well paid. (F 16)

His is the primitive concept that use gives him a claim on the land that supersedes even the owner's rights. Although there are echoes here of the landlord-peasant struggles, Bull's remarks arise from anger, hurt that his claim has not been honored, and fear that he might lose the field. The political and social facts of landlordism may form an historical frame for Bull's remarks about outsiders, but it is his personal possessiveness that emerges in his hatred for the stranger: "That's what I care about outsiders. Accursed friggers with nothing in their heads only to own the ground we're walkin' on. We had their likes long enough, hadn't we. Land is all that matters. Own your own land" (F 16). This statement both demonstrates Bull's position and foreshadows the arrival of William Dee who not only wishes to bid against McCabe but who plans to turn the field to commercial use.

The story of *The Field* is very simple. It concerns a widow, Maggie Butler, who wishes to sell her four-acre field. She instructs the publican and auctioneer, Mick Flanagan, to advertise a public auction and to sell that land at the highest possible price. While this seems to be a straightforward procedure, Flanagan and the regulars in the pub realize that Mrs. Butler's actions will disturb Bull McCabe who has been leasing the field for grazing. McCabe bribes the publican into keeping the auction secret so that no other bidders will come forward. He then will be able to offer the price he wants, and Maggie Butler will be forced to accept it. The conflict occurs when a stranger from England, William Dee, arrives to bid on the field. In the course of the bidding, it becomes clear that Dee will not be deterred from his intentions either by Flanagan's suggestions or McCabe's threats. The result is violence and death.

It is not only the thought of losing his grazing that angers Bull McCabe but also the thought, inconceivable to any Kerryman, that the stranger would cover the grass with concrete and use the field for the manufacture of concrete blocks. This is a key to McCabe's character. It is love for the land that makes him a Kerryman and less of a Stage Irish figure. John B. Keane summed up this reverence for the land during a conversation about the subjects of his plays. He spoke about his preference for subjects in which there are powerful values such as "the love a man has for land; for instance," and he continued:

> I've seen men love land the way they love women—kneeling on their knees and stroking the fleecy grass of a young meadow, or catching a fist of wheat in their hands and rubbing it and sniffing it. I've seen them going down to an oat field and stroke the sheaves, the stalks of oats, the way they'd stroke a young girl's hair, a daughter's hair or a wife's hair. . . . It transcends affection and it transcends love as we know it. It's a commitment to that which sustains them; it's sacrificial in a sense, and it's their way of responding to the nerves of nature. Nature doesn't speak, but it can communicate beautifully with people who appreciate it, and the seemingly inarticulate North Kerry farmer . . . has a greater relationship with nature than it is possible to define.[1]

This is Bull McCabe. While the audience is not asked to condone either the murder or the silence that protects him, we can understand that it is McCabe's inarticulate love that surfaces in his recitation of all he has done for the land, and he answers the fear of loss with his own weapon, violence. He hopes he can scare off all bids but his own by threatening William Dee. Failing in this, Bull and his son set out to intimidate the buyer with a beating, and the outcome of the midnight venture has been foreshadowed because the audience knows that Bull and Tadhg are responsible for the death of a donkey in the same field. Bull justifies the crime by reminding the people in the pub of the destructiveness of the animal and the loss of good grass. He continues by bragging about Tadhg's role in the killing and restates his claim to the field:

> The first time I met that stallion was a Stephen's Day and he staring through one of the gates of the field we're buying now. You'd think butter wouldn't melt in his mouth. To look at his face you'd think grass was the last thing in his head. He gave me a look and he trotted off. That night he broke the gate. Three months we watched him until we cornered him. Tadhg there beat him to death. He was a solid hour flaking him with his fists and me with a blackthorn. An' do

you mean to tell me I have no claim to this field? That any outside
stranger can make his open bid and do us out of what's ours, after
we huntin' every connivin' jackass from the countryside? (F 19)

This crime remains unsolved because of the silence of the townspeople, and the inference is clear. Both the killing of the donkey
and the action of the villagers prepare for the McCabes' murder
of the man who threatens their ownership of the land.

A marvelous juxtaposition of love and violence occurs in the
scene in which Bull and his potentially murderous son await
William Dee's arrival at the field. Bull speaks tenderly of the
season and the land: "'Tis April, boy, 'Tis April. Listen and you
can hear the first growth of the grass. The first music that was
ever heard. That was a good bit o' sun today. A few more days
like it and you won't know the face of the field" (F 47). Opposing
this description is the brief exchange in which Bull explains to
his son the eighteen years of bitterness in his marriage. He traces
his marital situation to the time when his wife allowed a tinker's
widow to turn a pony loose in a field that "was carryin' fourteen
cows an' grass scarce. Fourteen cows, imagine, an' to go throwin'
a pony in on top of them! Cripes, Tadhg, a tinker's pony would
eat the hair off a child's head!" (F 49). McCabe goes on to describe the manner in which he destroyed the animal, and one
realizes that even his family life has been sacrificed to his lust for
land. McCabe's poetic description of the grass seems an unlikely
speech from a scheming and violent man, yet, in the cultural
and psychological landscape which is the heart of a Kerryman,
there is sympathy for Bull in spite of his cheating and murder.

Keane directs his audience to appreciate the love for land that
recoils at the inroads of technology. No one in a North Kerry
dairy farming community would understand an individual's us-
ing land for any reason other than grazing. Mechanization is
abhorrent to the rural soul, and it destroys the individuality of
places. In a technological society every place is the same; characteristic differences have been eroded by standardization and
electronic communication. This is the aspect of The Field that
does not travel well; in urban areas, the kind of loyalty that binds
the villagers together would be unfamiliar, even anachronistic.
To an audience that has experienced only the modern, highly

mobile world, the demands of law would be favored over the love for land.

One could draw the obvious parallels between individual ownership of land and the political scene. The long memory of the Irish people carries the scars of landlordism and oppression. These are also part of the sense of place which gives another way of looking at the play. They are important to traditional interpretations of Irish fiction, but the political meanings are not essential to an appreciation of Bull McCabe as a Kerryman. The attitude toward the outsider is a characteristic of all rural communities as well as a reflection of Irish history. What makes this play specifically Keane's, and specifically modern, is his concern for Bull McCabe as an individual. As Father Murphy and the Sergeant leave the stage at the end of the play, still unsuccessful at proving McCabe's guilt, Bull calls after them:

> No, I won't face her because I seen her and she's a pretty bit and the grass won't be green over his grave when she'll take another man . . . a dead man is no good to anyone. Eh, Tadhg? That right? Eh, Maimie? *(They turn their faces from him. He sits down weakly.)* That's the way of the world. The grass won't be green over his grave when he'll be forgot by all . . . forgot by all except me! (F 76)

The final line suggests that the bravado of the bully covers some feelings of remorse. McCabe's dilemma speaks to the heart of the audience, and, supported by the other devices of the play, his love-hate bond with the land arouses the sympathy of the spectators.

The theatrical devices include the elements of characterization, setting, and language that locate the scene in Ireland, and specifically in North Kerry. One of the most interesting of these is the cross section of village life that passes through the pub, and, thereby, through the eyes of the audience. One meets the overworked mother, wife of the publican, and, through her, the double standard of Irish sexuality. She is tied to the pub by the demands of such premises and her nine children, yet when she does manage to get out for an evening, she suffers her husband's jealousy and suspicions. There are remarks which indicate that she may have irritated her husband by her flirtations, but there is no evidence of infidelity. Her relationship with her son Leamy demonstrates the mother-son bond in Irish families. Maimie praises and protects him; he, on his part, would not dream of disobeying his mother, yet he is troubled by her apparent approval of Bull McCabe's actions. After the murder, we learn that Leamy has been sent away because of a nervous breakdown. Whether the breakdown is real or whether he has been sent away because his father is unsure of his loyalty is never explored in the play. In the revised script, Leamy is the unseen observer of the final scene, and his mute presence suggests the communal bond of silence will continue. The other regulars in the public include "the Bird" O'Donnell, a sycophant and sponger, and a spectrum of local characters seen in relation to the publican and Bull McCabe. Each fills out a part of the Kerry landscape against which this story is enacted.

The story itself is true. It is based on an unsolved murder that occurred in the Stacks Mountains; it was a case in which a dispute over land precipitated the violence and in which the silence of the local residents hid the guilty parties from the authorities. This disdain for the legal system stems from the custom, which often flourishes in remote areas, whereby the locals dispense their own form of justice, based more on remnants of the Brehon code than on English law. Synge observed this spirit on the Aran Islands and incorporated the disregard for law into *The Playboy of the Western World*. The people welcome the fugitive Christy as a hero, but they turn against him when he tries to recommit the "crime" in their neighborhood. Although more prevalent in the West, the disdain for legal institutions, and a particular abhorrence for the informer, marks the attitude toward foreign law throughout the country. In some remote areas people have transferred to the Irish government the attitude they once had toward the Crown with the result that the police, the Gardai, are often looked upon as outsiders in rural communities. This is the case in *The Field* when the villagers protect the McCabes by refusing to cooperate with the investigation. Eileen Moriarty, in her study of Keane, traces the ambivalent attitude of Kerrymen toward the law to their failure to see a connection between law and morality. She notes that they tend to regard "the law as something against which they had to match their wits, or as something which at times could be utilized to their own advantage."[2] Thus the villagers in Keane's play transfer their distrust of alien law to the Police Sergeant and the Parish Priest. They will have their own way of punishing Bull, as the averted faces of Maimie and Tadhg suggest in the final scene, but they will not hand him over to the law.

The interrogation is a game of wits. The Police Sergeant and the Parish Priest have joined forces in the hope of extracting information from the regulars in Flanagan's pub. Keane's best dialogue records the Kerryman's skill at eluding any implication in the crime. In the cross-examination scene he captures the shrewdness and the individuality of the characters. Neither the appeal to law nor to God has any effect as each person responds to the questions in a self-interested manner. Maggie Butler speaks of the fears of an old woman living alone, and Maimie Flanagan turns her first answer into a joke: "All right! I confess everything! I killed him! I've said goodbye to the kids. *(Raises her hands over her head)* Take me, Sergeant!" (F 68). She affects a superficial grasp of the proceeding, as if she were unable to contribute to the investigation; however, her turning the focus of her remarks to her own situation is quite clever: "All right! So a man has been murdered! What's it to me. I've nine kids to look after. I wasn't at a picture in three years and I never go outside the door of this pub except when I go to Mass. Look at the state of me from cooking and scrubbing and scraping" (F 68). Her irritability sidetracks the investigation, but it is not counterfeit. Maimie is concerned for her children, particularly Leamy, and angry that she must agree with her husband and lie for Bull McCabe. Since she cannot combat McCabe's threats to their business, she directs her anger at her husband and those insensitive to her plight:

> Yes . . . but don't ask me what was said. A woman has a head like a sieve, and a woman expecting the tenth time should have her head examined! How well they wouldn't murder me! No such luck! I'll have to stay alive and look at thicks like you climbing on other people's backs because you have authority. (F 69)

During the questioning, "Bird" O'Donnell and the others continue to insist that Bull and Tadhg were in the pub at the time the murder was committed. The Bird repeats his testimony in the manner of a well-rehearsed speech, and Mick Flanagan protests his innocence by attacking the Sergeant:

Mick. . . . He'll go too far. He won't be the first Sergeant to be transferred. I always voted right.
Sergeant. I'm well aware of how you vote. Will you tell the Bird I
want him.
Mick. Very well. But hurry it up. What will the neighbours think,
the Sergeant and the priest here all the morning? 'Tis how they'll
think I'm the murderer.
Sergeant. Everybody knows that you didn't do it, Mick, because
everybody knows it was another man . . . maybe two men.
Mick. 'Tis your job to find out. (F 70)

The surface amenities, the cooperation of the villagers, cover
their antipathy for the law and their fear of McCabe. Justice is
not served, and McCabe sums up the poor man's attitude toward
the legal institutions as he angrily protests his innocence:

And, by God, it wasn't Bull McCabe and it wasn't Tadhg, and Tadhg
and me are sick of your dirty informer's tactics. You've been after us
now since the donkey was kilt. We're watching your shifty peeler's
questions. The two of you there have the power behind you. Why
isn't it some other man you picked, Sergeant, to go searching with
you? Like the labourer, or the servant boy? Why wasn't it a plough-
man or a Council worker? No . . . you picked one of the gang. If
'twasn't the priest 'twould be the doctor or the schoolmaster or the
well-off shopkeeper. You have the law well sewn up, all of you . . .
all nice and tidy to yourselves. (F 74)

Bull's attitude toward the law illustrates the separation between
the ordinary laborer and the professional class in the village.
The distinction dates from the time when the priest, the doctor,
and the schoolteacher were the only educated individuals in the
rural areas. The farming community recognizes a subtle split
between the two groups even today, and as *The Field* demonstrates, a crisis finds the people and the institutions on opposing sides.

This evidence of class distinction is another avenue leading to
an appreciation of the social context of North Kerry. Both the
Law and the Church are outsiders in Keane's play. Because the
Sergeant and Father Murphy, along with the murdered man, do
not belong to the fellowship of the rural laborers, they cannot be
intimidated by Bull's threats. Nor do they have the trust of the
villagers which would give them access to the information they
request. The position of the Church here may be more of a sur-

prise than the villagers' reaction toward the police. Historically, the clergy has exercised considerable influence in the daily life of Irish Catholics. The tales in William Carleton's *Traits and Stories* and George Moore's *The Untilled Field* present views of the Church that both illustrate the leadership of the Parish Priest in moral and political matters, and, at the same time, attack the repressive aspects of their control. Because the Church, like all institutions, flourishes in a stable political environment, it has been seen at times as an arm of the civil authority. For example, many of Parnell's supporters attributed his fall from power and the defeat of Home Rule to the Church's stance on divorce. Since the present Irish constitution safeguards the official position of the Church, the role of the institutional Church in public life sometimes appears as remote as government in the life of the average Irishman. What becomes clear in *The Field* is a subtle distinction between personal religious practice and the individual's perception of the institution. Bull's outburst against the law and the Parish Priest also contains his recollection of an old poor priest who had visited him and talked about "hard luck, about dead-born calves and the cripples you meet among dropped calves" (F 74). The McCabes clearly feel that the simple old priest is one of them, but they infer that Father Murphy is out of touch with the concerns of the ordinary parishioners.

Except in the matter of the law, there is no direct criticism of the Church in Keane's play; however, suggestions that the Church is not an effective part of the daily life of the people are very evident. The structure of the play and the language of both the Bishop and the Parish Priest separate them from the mainstream of village life. The Bishop's sermon is certainly the kind of appeal the spiritual leader of the people should make. Even his threats of interdict are appropriate to his authority. The striking thing about the Bishop as a character is that he appears in the pulpit but is never portrayed interacting directly with other persons in the play. This may have been a decision based on problems of production and not a deliberate comment on the relevance of religion; however, the Bishop's position in *The Field* suggests a minor role for Church authority in contemporary Ireland. Not only does his language distance him from the ordinary people, but the scene in the pulpit is also one of only two scenes set in a locale other than the pub; the other is the murder scene.

Both the murder and the sermon occur outside the villagers' daily life. From the gossip in the pub one learns that the values are self-centered, and neither violence nor admonitions effectively influence them.

The separation of the Bishop's instruction from the ordinary routine divides the two spheres of religious belief and moral practice. The Bishop and the murdered man are both outside the enclosure of the community, and, therefore, not entitled to the same loyalty. Although *The Field* raises a doubt about the actions of the townspeople and the failure of justice, Keane does not provide a solution to current social problems. His references to technological improvements—electricity, television, cosmetics, and jet planes—are frequent enough for the audience to recognize its own world and to be shocked by the harshness of the conditions. *The Field* may seem to be a primitive and traditional story of land-greed, but the allusions remind the audience that it is set in contemporary Ireland. Keane proposes that two rules govern the rural community, the Ten Commandments and self-preservation, but he does not condemn those who fail. He treats his characters with great compassion because they are caught between the demands of the two laws. He directs the audience, through an understanding of the sense of place, toward the recognition that there are no simple answers even in questions of murder. Bull McCabe will be punished, as the final lines suggest, but he will be subject to the justice of the community not the disposition of urban institutions. *The Field* is in many ways a traditional rural drama. When Keane sets the question of land-greed in his own time, he causes his contemporaries to consider social conditions in modern Ireland.

The Field offers a pessimistic view of Irish rural life, and its counterpart *Big Maggie* presents a similar picture of a country town. In *Big Maggie*, Keane treats the need for financial security and personal fulfillment. The play opens with the burial of Maggie Polpin's husband and depicts her assuming control of the family business and the lives of her adult children. Like Bull McCabe, Maggie Polpin is a larger-than-life figure, a character that does not arouse sympathy immediately, although one tends to attribute her hardness to her unhappy marriage. She has experienced both frustrations and embarrassment, but her response appears unnecessarily harsh. The audience sees her bitterness and her resolve that no one will take advantage of her again and concurs with Byrne's observation: "We would need softer stone than you, Maggie" (BM 15). An understanding of her character, even of her hardness, comes only after one has examined her situation in the context of the cultural landscape. Maggie Polpin systematically imposes her own sense of order on the shop and on the lives of her children, and her sons and daughters leave home in order to escape her control. While her methods appear cruel, a closer look at Maggie's character reveals both the stereotypes against which she is rebelling and the social implications suggested by the playwright.

Maggie may be one of those strong women in Irish literature in whom sex, religion, and maternal instincts combine to represent a distinctive part of the Irish consciousness. In contrast, some readers may find a feminist statement in Keane's heroine. Actually, both of these views contribute to an interpretation of Maggie's character. Irish women of the past and the changing society join to establish the place in which Maggie lives. Her actions reflect both her certitude about traditional values and her criticism of the norms that have enslaved her. Maggie Polpin is both a rebel and a dictator. Freed by her husband's death from the restrictions imposed by society, she refuses to show even the outward trappings of grief at his funeral. When her daughter protests, Maggie asserts, "I could paint a picture of your late, lamented father that would really shock you! I rejected him utterly many years ago when you were a little girl but like all wives, I kept my mind to myself. Pride and ignorance and religion! Those were the chains around me so I stayed put and sang dumb" (BM 17). The elements of pride, ignorance, and religion—the chains as she calls them—provide clues to the popularity of this play in Ireland and its failure to be fully appreciated abroad. They represent aspects of the cultural landscape that would prescribe and regulate the Irish woman's role in the family and society. Rigid morality and gossip enforce the social codes of all small towns. Irish society adds the demands of self-sacrifice to the expectations of virtue. Both tradition and religion, therefore, laud the woman who accepts hardships and sacrifices her own interests for the good of her husband and children. The resulting conventions form a code of conduct against which Irish women's actions can be judged. This is the same code about which Maimie

Flanagan remarks in *The Field* when she speaks bitterly of the intrusions of the local community in her life: "If you get your hair done different, they whisper about you. Dress up in a bit of style and they stare at you. You'd want an armoured car if you wore a pair of slacks. They know the month you start expecting (F 14). Both religious practice and community gossip keep the women of Maimie and Maggie's generation in their proper roles. This is the "sense of place" that underlies Maggie's understanding of her new position as widow and authority in the family.

There is something of the avatar of Ireland in the traditional Irish woman—the nourishing mother who sacrifices herself and asks only loyalty from her children. But Maggie Polpin is neither Cathleen ni Houlihan nor Juno Boyle. She welcomes the opportunity of casting aside the role assigned her by convention, and she forces her children to become independent as well. She is not like Stephen Dedalus's mother who haunts his memory and binds him by her love and the "nets" of national and religious institutions. Instead, Maggie alienates her children, and, although she expects them to thank her eventually, there is no indication in the play that they appreciate her "hardness of concern" (BM 81).

Barry Cassin, who directed the original production, calls *Big Maggie* the greatest theatrical success in Irish history. In an interview with this writer, he remembered the play as "outrageously funny" and an "explosive experience." Such an impact must be due, in part, to Maggie's familiarity to the audience. Cassin recalls that the character generated comments that ranged from "outrageous character" to "she's like me aunt,"[3] and Christopher Murray, of University College Dublin, suggests that the audience cheers Maggie's courage in the face of provincial tyranny.[4] Within the play itself, the spokesman for the playwright's concept of Maggie appears to be Byrne, an engraver of monuments and a man of property. He would like to marry Maggie, but she has no interest in a second marriage. Byrne's presence as commentator provides a view of Maggie which is both realistic and sympathetic. He remarks on her hardness, but as the play progresses he appears to grasp her reasons for being hard, although she is as harsh with him as with her children.

Each scene presents a facet of her relationship with her family. Her son Mick leaves home very early in the play because he is disappointed in his hope of inheriting the farm, and Katie marries in order to escape Maggie's domination. Gert turns to nursing after her mother has disrupted her plans for an evening with the commercial traveler. Maurice remains to work the family farm and expects that Maggie will eventually permit him to marry the girl of his choice; his dreams are thwarted by his mother's insistence on a large dowry. Byrne seems to understand both sides when he speaks with Maurice. He expresses his understanding of Maggie, and he urges the young man to be independent:

> Your mother is like strong medicine—hard to take some times but 'twill do you good in the long run.
>
> . . . .
>
> If I was in your shoes, Maurice, I'd learn how to lace them myself and not have my mother always tying them for me. (BM 64)

Maggie's motives would be clear to an Irish audience; some would see in her stance an action they themselves lacked the courage to try. They would appreciate her desire for independence and her determination to free her children from reliance on the family inheritance. The audience would find Maggie's actions both drastic and humorous. They would laugh at her trapping of the commercial traveler and applaud her intentions although her methods also place her at odds with her society at the time when she is most vigorously defending the rights of individuals within that society. Maggie may be similar to the strong women in Irish drama, but her quest for power serves her own ends, not family or social goals. Family is as important an element of place as the physical landscape, but Maggie chooses to disregard the expected modes of behavior and asserts her own individuality in defiance of both her family and the community. In the opening scene, she reminds Byrne and the audience that "there's enough lies written on the headstones of Ireland without my adding to them" (BM 15), and her subsequent actions continue to run counter to the expectations of her society.

There is a playful interaction between normal behavior and caricature in *Big Maggie*. The scene in the final act in which Maggie threatens Mrs. Madden with a shotgun seems melodramatic, perhaps anachronistic; however, a shotgun would be an ordinary implement in a country home in the era of the play.

Barry Cassin explains that he chose that piece of business because it was consistent with the time and setting of the play and consistent also with Maggie's defense of her son's independence.[5] While the shotgun might be appropriate to the setting, Maggie's reaction to her son's impregnating Mary Madden is not. Convention would have demanded a "shotgun" wedding, not a denial of responsibility. Maggie attacks the girl and her family as opportunists instead of agreeing to the marriage which local attitudes would have prescribed. It is in situations like this that the criticism of Irish society surfaces. While Maggie Polpin endorses traditional Catholic morality when she vehemently denounces Katie's affair with a married man, she also recognizes that the power of puritanical opinion could trap her son in an undesirable marriage. Maggie's attitude offends both her son and the Maddens because she does not do the expected thing. In this case, as in her flirtation with the commercial traveler and her sharpness with Katie, she acts in the interests of her children. Neither her children nor her neighbors, however, recognize her true intentions. Society considers only her flaws, that is, her apparent selfishness and her abrasive disregard for family name and social convention.

It is Byrne alone who permits the audience a glimpse of the true character of Maggie Polpin. In the first scene, he is speaking to a few townspeople at the cemetery and comments that although the deceased had his faults, "Still I liked him. She was wrong for him. Another woman might have made a better fist of him. 'Tis a mistake to fight fire with fire" (BM 22). Coming shortly after Maggie has told Gert that she had rejected her husband many years before, this speech offers a clue to Maggie's hardness. Because she punishes her husband's infidelity by refusing him affection, Maggie has repressed her own sexuality and become a callous, bitter-tongued woman. Byrne laments her choice and later remarks that "She was all right at first. 'Twas the world hardened her" (BM 23). This notion of the hardness of the world continues as a motif in Maggie's description of her own actions.

As Maggie speaks on the importance of self-respect (BM 69), she is confident that her children will thank her eventually because she has made them self-reliant and spared them some of the mistakes she herself has made. She tells Teddy Heelin that Gert will learn from her embarrassment:

> She'll get over it, she won't travel the same road I did. You won't get the chance to treat her like the dirt under your feet. She'll think twice before she falls for your kind again. That's exactly what happened to me. The man I married lived exactly the way you are living now. When we married everyone said he'd change, but he didn't change. If anything he was worse. (BM 68)

Maggie is convinced that her hardness is the best education that her children will receive; it is the only thing, she claims, that will prepare them for the world in which they must live.

Maggie herself sums up the entire play in her words: "'Tis the hardness of concern. Always remember that about me" (BM 81). The words, however, appear to be lost on her children, who are consumed by the hurt of Maggie's treatment. They have neither the experience nor the wisdom to appreciate her motives:

> *Katie.* Have you any feeling at all for me?
> *Maggie.* How can you ask that, when you know I saved you from disgrace?
> *Katie.* But have you any feeling of love for me?
> *Maggie.* I have! I have it for all of you. That's why I never let any of you have your own way. If I hadn't love I wouldn't care. (BM 83)

Neither Katie nor Maurice is able to see beyond the present, and they leave Maggie alone with her convictions. Only Byrne is able to approach her with thoughts of loneliness:

> *Byrne.* They've all gone from you now, but maybe that's the way you wanted it.
> *Maggie.* Maybe. But isn't it natural, Byrne, that the birds should leave the nest when they're fledged. If I left them here they'd turn into four dictators before long.
> *Byrne.* You're hard, Maggie.
> *Maggie.* I thank God that I am, Byrne! I'm independent now and I'm entitled to be. The hardship of the world will harden my children and they'll have regard for me yet. (BM 93)

The final scene with Byrne has been deleted from the revision of *Big Maggie* in which Brenda Fricker played the title role. In the new ending, Maggie sits alone, after her encounter with the

Maddens, and reflects on her experiences and her opportunities. The image of Maggie alone on stage forms a parenthesis with the opening scene in which she is sitting on a tombstone. There has, however, been a significant change.[6] Keane uses the soliloquy to summarize the sexual and moral climate of 1950s Ireland. Maggie exults in her new freedom and outlines the struggles and frustrations of her married life. She laments her ignorance and the lack of guidance in sexual matters and blames the social landscape of her youth where "My sex life, my morals, my thought, word and deed were dominated by a musty old man with a black suit and a roman collar and a smell of snuff" (Three 234). Her long speech attacks both her late husband and the moral and social code of Ireland, and Maggie charts for herself a future in which "there's still time to fulfil myself" (Three 235).

The new ending has aroused some controversy in both literary and theatrical circles. Some like Dr. Christopher Murray of University College Dublin feel that the final speech is a vehicle for a strong actress but not consistent with the character of Maggie as it unfolds in the play.[7] Others, notably Gus Smith, suggest that Brenda Fricker had too much influence with the playwright and the director. He remarks that the acting community found the ending self-indulgent. Smith agreed, however, that Barnes's staging of Big Maggie was memorable and that the frame of Maggie alone on stage at the beginning and end gave the character great authority. He does find some contradictions in the play and contends that, while taking a fresh look at a play is often a good thing, it was not wise of Keane to change his original intentions and overstate the moral and social causes of Maggie's situation.[8]

Ben Barnes defends the revision of Big Maggie by noting that the earlier version reflects a time in which many things were left unsaid because of political and religious custom. He admits that he and Brenda Fricker asked Keane to consider what more could be said since the restraints no longer exist. Thus the new ending was developed.[9] Keane agrees that Maggie has been shedding her restrictions and problems throughout the play and contends that the criticism of the ending is unwarranted. Keane tends to resent the reactions of scholars and suggests that their calling has made them "too refined. . . . too sheltered from real life."[10]

The play is not a woman's liberation piece, although the new ending comes close to pushing the work in that direction. It is a play about relationships, and Maggie's need to control her children for their own good. This focus remains whether one approves of the new ending or not. Maggie continues to assail the tradition of Irish motherhood that works for the comfort and success of the children without exacting any repayment. The result of such sacrifice, Maggie says, is that the children become demanding "dictators" much like the husband whose word was law. Maggie prefers the hardness of concern to the softness that will make her children dependent on her for the rest of their lives. There is merit in sacrifice, certainly, in the Catholic tradition; there is spiritual strength to be gained from suffering. Maggie recognizes that the attitude also has a negative side, however, a passivity whereby women rarely become molders of their own destinies. This is the modern woman emerging in Keane's heroine. Maggie subscribes to the traditional moral code of marriage and sexual relationships, but she sees that her responsibility to her adult children is to set them free, to anger them, if necessary, into asserting their own independence from her. She herself admits that when she's gone, they will inherit the land and whatever else she has (BM 93), but, in the meantime, she prefers them to learn self-reliance even if the school is hard.

It is difficult to sympathize with Maggie, and this writer wrestled with the harshness of her character until both Barry Cassin, director of the original production, and the playwright suggested that the phrase "hardness of concern" epitomizes both the character and the play.[11] In this context, Byrne becomes a commentator who shows Maggie's attitudes and actions in their appropriate perspective. His remarks focus on the necessity that changed maternal concern into determination and hardness. In many ways Maggie and Mena Glavin are alike: Necessity has hardened both of them, but they differ in the cause and the nature of their behavior. Mena has suffered physical deprivation, and her own need for food, clothing, and security determines her attitude toward Sive and her insistence on the arranged marriage. Maggie has money, but, as Keane says, "She was nurtured on hardship by a tyrannical, unloving and wandering husband."[12] Her goal is to spare her children the dependence on others that she has endured. Byrne's summation, in the original, "I can't say you're right and I can't say you're wrong" (BM 93), reminds one of the compassion with which Keane treats Bull McCabe. In the revised version, Maggie speaks for herself and against the religious and social contraints that forced her to endure a loveless, unfilling marriage. Ultimately, Maggie represents Keane's concern for the freedom of women, and she differs from other strong female characters in Irish drama because she acts for herself and not for the good of the community.

The social dilemma of the modern Irish woman, faced with traditional expectations and growing feminism, cannot be completely explored in one play, but John B. Keane provides a glimpse of the modern woman in a rural, conservative setting. Her dilemma is not moral, but social. At risk here is the family name, for those who subvert the time-honored practices, even for a greater good, must pay the price of misunderstanding and loneliness. Keane's gift is the humor which makes Maggie recognizable to all, shocking to some, and a mystery to American audiences for whom the character belongs to an earlier period, not to contemporary drama. A sense of Maggie's cultural and social milieu is essential to an understanding of this play. The past is still very much alive in the Irish consciousness, and, although there has been urban development and technological advancement, Ireland is essentially a rural nation. An appreciation of place in the plays of John B. Keane depends both on a grasp of the influences from the past and an understanding of the ways in which new ideas are received in a rural environment.

7

Separation from the Land

The Field and *Big Maggie* are companion pieces that control between them the range of John B. Keane's theatrical output. The themes of economic security and sexual frustration create the "place" in which he examines contemporary Irish life. By setting his portrayals of Kerry against the background of puritanical attitudes and land-greed, Keane shows that emigration, conflicts between generations, and struggles for power are motifs deeply rooted in the Irish consciousness. No longer subject to Nationalist censorship, modern playwrights express their search for identity by examining the conditions of Irish society. John B. Keane and others continue to draw on the communal heritage, but their primary concern is the ordinary person who is coping with traditional values in a changing society. Keane criticizes the institutions that have exerted the greatest influence on the populace: the Catholic Church and the Irish government. He contends that institutions are remote from ordinary experience and the individual struggle. Keane points out their flaws as an insider, and, like Maggie's hardness, his is a criticism of concern. Both friends and critics of John B. Keane agree that he does not set out to convey a message in his plays, but in drawing on the daily life of rural people, as he knows it, he has provided a series of social documents while entertaining his public.

Land and family are so evidently elements of place in the Irish consciousness that themes such as emigration and repressed sexuality are always related to issues of inheritance and name. In many of Keane's rural plays the themes cannot be separated; they form the fabric of life in a country setting in which status in the community is determined more by family than by one's personal attributes. This study has already examined power struggles in Bull's land-greed and Maggie's assertion of personal independence. Power struggles also motivate the action in *Sive* and *Sharon's Grave*, and, in many of Keane's plays, parallel themes of marriage and sexual repression are linked to the obsession with security and land. While Keane sometimes uses grotesque images from folk memory to describe unnatural sexuality, as in *Sharon's Grave*, he more often roots the personal frustrations of his characters in their family relationships. Thus, both Maggie and Bull suffer in their marriages, and Mena's childlessness is as much a cause of her actions toward Sive as her greed.

Historically, the question of land in Irish literature was a political one, and owning land was the expression of one's natural rights as an individual and as a nation. Some contemporary writers wrap the individual frustrations stemming from authority, rigid moral codes, censorship, and the lure of the cities in the traditional themes. For these authors, the struggle for identity, once symbolized by the land alone, is embodied also in motifs of failed authority and sexual mores. Certainly, the sufferings of an individual may be emblematic of the nation, or of the world, but John B. Keane's first concern is always the individual struggle. Therefore, as Keane celebrates the life of a country town and the variety of its characters, one of his chief themes is that men and women ought to find security in their own region. For him, emigration is a tragedy for the person and for the nation; he blames both family greed and the government for the conditions which force so many young people to go abroad in search of work.

Several of Keane's plays have dealt with the motif of emigration probably because of his own experience. He records his journey from home and his years in England in *Self-Portrait*, but his plays depict his feelings even more poignantly. Both *Hut 42* and *No More in Dust* portray conditions in the factories and boarding houses of the urban areas. *Hut 42* depicts the life of six men in a hostel near a construction site in northern England, dramatizing both the hardship of the labor and the loneliness of the emigrants. It is a melancholy play about the workers' longing to return to Ireland. While *Hut 42* is not one of Keane's best plays, it is a realistic picture of the laborer's lot and the gradual dying of his personal ambition and his hope of returning home. The strong characterizations carry the intensity of feeling which one expects when Keane writes about exile. When addressing Ildris, the Welsh laborer, Bill Root sums up his own position and the plight of all emigrants:

> We don't want much in Ireland but they won't even give us that little much. What do an old man like me want . . . a bit o' meat for his dinner, a fire an' a bed. That's not too much . . . but it's not a labourin' man's country back there. He has no power like they have here. He's no better than the ground he walks on in Ireland. They'll have to get jobs for the fathers o' families back there, or have they any notion of the way they're behavin' here? Can you blame a married man if he gets lonely on the Saturday night an' goes prowlin' for company? (H 19)

This authentic portrait of an aging migrant worker is Keane's firm, but loving, reproof of the governmental system that permits such conditions to continue. Its companion piece *No More in Dust* received mixed reviews during the Dublin Theatre Festival of 1961. Gabriel Fallon writes that "Mr. Keane's play was a competent piece of dramaturgy concerning the love life of country girls in Dublin lodgings."[1] Despite its apparent failure, the play testifies to Keane's particular interest in the problem of emigration, which he treats with great success in *Many Young Men of Twenty*.

This is a lively play wherein the characterization of necessity and greed is heightened by the music, particularly the haunting title song, which introduces the motifs of emigration and lost youth. Here, as in many of Keane's other plays, the action involves several related situations, each exemplifying a facet of the major theme. Central to his purpose is the story of the young men and women who gather in the backroom of Tom Hannigan's public house on the day of their departure for England. Another view of the theme comes from villagers, like Peg Finnerty and Tom Hannigan, who feel that their chances for a new life have passed. Unlike the young, who set out in fear but with dreams of success, these characters lament their lost opportunities. *Many Young Men of Twenty*, although it deals specifically with emigration, also dramatizes the death of youth and idealism.

Kevin and Dinny, the sons of Daheen Timmineen Din, represent the large numbers of young people who left Ireland in the fifties and sixties because there was no work for them at home. Keane portrays their innocence and their eagerness, and, by allowing us to see the same boys on their first visit home, he depicts the change in their dreams as a serious loss. This is more than the loss of innocence; Keane finds that the young people from the country are swallowed up by the impersonal atmosphere of urban living. Through the character of Danger Mullaly, he comments on their becoming anonymous faces in a crowd. Separated from their roots, from the villages where they are well known, the exiles suffer a loss of identity. Consequently, they never return, or, if they do, they never belong again. Thus, one can understand the prejudice that greeted William Dee, a returning exile, in *The Field.* This type of intolerance from the community is another facet of the emigrant's situation. Keane suggests that the structures of Irish society frustrate people instead of freeing them to be themselves.

Many Young Men of Twenty provides an example in the character of Dinny. In the opening scene, he is an eighteen-year-old frightened and tearful at the prospect of leaving home, even though his brother is with him. He seems vulnerable, fearful both of his father and of the new life to which his father is sending him. One year later, Dinny returns with city clothes, a Cockney accent, and an English wife. Not only are his clothes and speech different, but his swagger and his drinking also proclaim him a changed man (Many 28). His childhood is gone and with it whatever hopes and ideals he once possessed. This, in Keane's view, is the most serious evil of emigration, an outcome which he himself escaped since he returned permanently to Kerry after only three years in England. The firmness of his conviction that the solution to the problem lies in Ireland can be seen in Keane's appeal in *Self-Portrait:*

> If there is an artist in this country—a real artist who wants to capture the truth for eternity on his canvases—my advice to him is to go to the North Wall, to Dun Laoghaire, to Rosslare or to Cork. Watch the faces, and unless you're a heartless inhuman moron, you'll feel something and your conscience will begin to bother you. I have been accused on several occasions of highlighting the problem of emigration and of evading the issue of a solution. The solution is—don't go! Stay at home. We are your people and this is your country. (SP 34–35)

Keane places the blame for the draining away of Irish youth on the economic condition of the country, and while he blasts the greed of the parents in this play, he also has sharp words for the government. Danger Mullaly, a colorful character who frequents Hannigan's, provides the author's viewpoint on the situation. The arrival of Daheen Timmineen Din and his family at the pub sets the context for Danger's commentary, when the father and sons recite the admonitions that parents have given their children through the years. Daheen's song places more emphasis on money than on their behavior; Kevin and Dinny repeat his advice as if committing it to memory:

> D.T.D. When you go to London town, work like Maggie May like Mikey Joe, send home the dough Let no week pass without your father's fiver, Rise at first light, stay home at night, And never ate black puddings of a Friday.
> Kevin and Dinny (singing) We'll do all the things you say We'll work day and night. On each pay day we'll kneel and pray And send our poor old father home his fiver And we declare, we hereby swear We'll never ate black puddin's of a Friday. (Many 7)

The songs remind the audience of the large numbers who emigrate from the farms to the cities or to England every year. Danger suggests quite strongly that greed has supplanted economic necessity in Daheen Timmineen Din's heart so that he, and many others, send their children out in order to reduce expenses at home:

> How many sons is he sending to England to-day? (counts) . . . One' . . . Two . . . (to himself) Two! . . . How many has he there before? . . . Approximately seven with daughters included. A wise investment (to the two boys) Did he tell ye to send home a pound or two every week to your poor father and mother? Did he tell ye not to forget the starvin' people at home, rearin' what's left of ye? (Kevin and Dinny exchange glances) Did he tell ye the trouble he has to make ends meet an' how his bones are fettered with hunger from shortages of money an the deadly struggle he had supportin' ye? Take a good look, boys, at yeer Da and Ma! Is there a tear on their faces? Is their hearts broke? Did ye ever in all the shortness of yeer lives see a brace of dog-bucketin', cat huntin', cantankerous curiosities? (Many 8)

At first one might distrust Danger Mullaly's remarks. He is, after all, one of the undesirables that Seelie Hannigan tries to keep away from the pub, just as she tries to control Tom's drinking.

Yet the audience also recognizes the stifling atmosphere which
Seelie creates, and Daheen convicts himself when he describes
his farm. Danger, for all his faults, is an astute judge. Seelie and
Daheen Timminneen Din betray the prejudice and greed that
contribute to emigration. Other characters, such as Peg and Kitty,
also feel the effects of the social structures; however, their responses differ. Some remain in Ireland because of their individual temperaments or responsibilities, but they lose heart. They
realize their failed opportunities, and it is likely that their future
will be to perpetuate the very structures that have hurt them.
Either they will become rigid examples of the social virtues or
they will escape by assuming antisocial postures. Others, like
Tom and Danger, try to salvage something of their future by leaving, although they lament the conditions that pressure them. As
Keane paints the picture in *Many Young Men of Twenty*, there
are few choices.

While the playwright uses strong words to describe the greed
of parents who send their children abroad, his attack on the
government is even stronger. The third act begins with another
family scene in the pub. This time, J. J. Houlihan, a local T.D.
(member of parliament), and his son Johnny await the train that
will take the boy to his new job in the north of the country. The
senior Houlihan prides himself on being a nephew of Mikey
Houlihan—the subject of Danger's song; however, while he
claims his uncle as a hero, Danger protests that the man died
by accident. In the course of the conversation between Maurice
Brown, the schoolmaster, and the Houlihans, it becomes clear
that Johnny has been appointed rate collector while six more
qualified men were not considered. Brown's outburst provides
us with Keane's view of the political system which rewards favor-
ites and sends so much talent and youth to other countries:

> You have the same politics as your father before you, and your sons
> after you will have the same politics. That's this damn country all
> over. You're all blinded by the past. You're still fighting the Civil War.
> Well, we don't give a tinker's curse about the Civil War or your damn
> politics, or the past. The future we have to think about. If there was
> any honest politician, he'd be damned. If our Lord walked down the
> main street of Keelty tomorrow morning, ye'd crucify him again.
> We're sick to death of hypocrisy and the glories of the past. Keep the
> Irish language and find jobs for the lads that have to go to England.

Forget about the Six Counties and straighten out the twenty-six first. (Many 37–38)

Although Johnny Houlihan is a weak character, there is hope for the future generations in his realization that others were more qualified than he. His words, when his father is not present, indicate his own preferences: "Don't want that job at all! The man that should have got it is a married man with two kids. I've my fare for England and that's where I'm going" (Many 38). From time to time, Keane allows his younger characters a moment in the spotlight in which they express opinions differing from those of their parents. Stalder, in his analysis of *The Field*, suggests that this is Keane's way of illustrating his own hope for the future in spite of present conditions.[2] There is slim evidence for this position in the plays. Keane's attitude toward the conditions that promote emigration generates biting condemnation. It is likely that the youthful disagreement is a realistic portrayal of idealism and the normal clashes between the generations.

The political situation that this play touches is one of the tender spots of twentieth-century Irish history. For a number of years after independence, Ireland followed an isolationist policy, and the leaders campaigned for an "Irish" Ireland totally separate from any English influence. While such a program is understandable in view of Ireland's history, it cut the island nation off from economic and technological development. Many levels of human living were touched by the onus of national pride so that religion, language, literature, and even sports were joined to the political ideal. Often, in searching in the Gaelic past for national identity, modern Ireland was smothered by the restrictions of history. Keane suggests, in the character of the T.D., that the ideals of the 1916 uprising and the subsequent Civil War have become lip service to an "Irish" Ireland while ordinary people are at the mercy of a new crowd of landlords.

Embellishing the legends of heroes is only one way of living in the past, but the play proposes that modern Irish leaders cater to an ideal that probably never existed rather than address the problems of the real world. The playwright does show that Tom Hannigan finally makes an attempt at breaking away from the structures of family and society. Danger also sets out for England because, as he tells Peg, he is lonesome, and he is looking forward to a job and fair treatment (Many 38). His farewell speeches both praise the job he is going to and blast the conditions that force the young into exile. Danger's words to Daheen Timmineen Din repeat his earlier sentiments: "So you're sendin' another shipment this mornin'. 'Tis worse than the horse trade" (Many 43), and he concludes by attacking the political situation that fails to do anything about emigration:

> We'll always be goin' from this miserable country. No one wants us. There's your Ireland for you, with grief and goodbyes and ullagoning at every Railway station. *(Passionately)* What honest-to-God politician with an ounce of guts in him would keep his mouth shut when he sees the father of a family goin' away alone with his heart broke, leavin' his poor children behind him. 'Tis the end of the world for them because their father is leavin' them behind. What man, with a drop o' honest blood in his veins, wouldn't rise up an' shout: "Stop! Stop it! Stop this cruelty. Stop tearin' the hearts out of innocent people! Stop sittin' down on yeer backsides an' do somethin'!" (Many 43–44)

Not only do the father figures Daheen Timmineen Din and J. J. Houlihan provide a context for Keane's denunciation of greed, they represent also the failure of leadership which is part of the conflict between the generations in modern Irish literature. The failed father is often an expression of the contemporary writer's preoccupation with the inadequacy of civil and religious institutions. He is also a central figure in stories dealing with the breakup of family life as the result of contemporary social pressures. Hiker Lacey is one example of the failure of male authority. In *The Year of the Hiker*, however, there is an attempt at reconciliation. Both Daheen and J. J. Houlihan are too far removed from their children; although physically present, they exercise authority by fear. In other Keane plays, for example, *The Crazy Wall*, the father avoids responsibility by embarking on a project instead of confronting real issues. The playwright suggests that failure to come to grips with reality contributes as much to the disintegration of Irish society as emigration. Keane's later plays look at personal frustration and isolation from family and community as characteristic of contemporary life, and, while he does not advocate a return to the past, he does lament the erosion of traditional values. The changes Keane cites are separations from the cultural landscape just as certainly as emigration or loss of land.

Although the building of a wall suggests a symbolic reading of the play, Keane's *The Crazy Wall* is a realistic and forceful portrayal of isolation. The central action depicts Michael Barnett's efforts at building a wall in order to ward off tramps and other intruders. His friend Jack hints at broader consequences, but Michael insists that he has no alternative:

> *Jack.* One wall could lead to another if you know what I mean.
> *Michael.* I don't know what you mean.
> *Jack.* You build a wall. You give everybody else a licence to do the same. Soon the whole street will be full of walls. You build a wall and you keep out Hanratty's hens. You shut out stray asses, mules and horses but you also shut yourself in. Building a wall is a very serious matter. I'll concede you'll keep out undesirables. You'll have more peace and privacy but you'll also be shutting out certain other things. (CW 18)

Barnett's determination about the wall is very quickly seen to be in marked contrast to his failure to take a firm stand with his sons Tom and Paddy. In spite of his wife's insistence that "one day it will be too late" for punishment (CW 23), Michael shifts his disappointment in his sons to a criticism of their teachers: "For the life of me I don't know how some of these fellows got into the Church, bloody refugees from the troubles of the world, hidden behind the smoke-screen of Holy Orders" (CW 25). His indictment of the clergy is a good description of his own mode of action; Michael Barnett never confronts an issue with his wife or sons. He turns to his cronies and to drink in order to soothe the hard times and to avoid his responsibilities. Ultimately, the wall is a symbol of all the failures of communication that the play illustrates. His son Lelum is the first to suggest that Michael is hiding from the real world, and his wife tries to remind him of his duty toward his sons:

> You are their father and it's your duty to drive them, to bully them, to forge them into men. You should be completely in command but you're not and they know you're not. (CW 43)
> . . . .
> Sometimes you make me sick. You close your eyes when there's a problem. Honestly there are times when I'm disgusted with you. You leave all the dirty work to me. I have to worry about the bills, about the future, about everything. When things get difficult you go and

build a wall. That's your answer when your family really needs firm direction. (CW 45)

Mary Barnett is concerned that her younger sons are so different from other boys, and her remarks could lead to another interpretation of the wall. The problems of communication in this play exist between husband and wife, father and sons, and the walls between them are representative of other separations in the larger community. The character of Moses McCoy, the wanderer, is a figure of an individual's ultimate separation from the norms of society and Church. Beneath the domestic tension of the play are the conflicts of World War II, which the voice of Lord Haw Haw keeps before the audience. One needs only to recall Ireland's isolation from the rest of Europe during that war in order to assign another level of meaning to the wall.

The breaking of the wall in the final scene coincides with the break-up of the family, and the sons do not come together again until their father's funeral. While this is Keane's only use of a controlling device to represent human frustrations, he does explore the failure of communication through other examples of spiritual exile. His later plays tend to focus on spiritual and psychological realities rather than on the physical struggles for land or money.

Two plays that prominently display the human condition are *Moll* and *The Chastitute*. Both deal with human limitations, a sort of spiritual greed, and both draw the strength of their characterizations from the prominence of certain types in the Irish scene. The Parish Priest's housekeeper and the aging bachelor are figures that are very familiar to the Irish audience—so familiar that the roles are close both to tragedy and to stage Irish stereotypes. Both plays present a view of the Catholic Church in Irish life. *Moll* examines the remoteness of the parish leadership from the daily experience of the people; *The Chastitute* satirizes the repressive influence of a puritanical clergy. Moll displays another aspect of the quest for identity in which power substitutes for land and family, while John Bosco McLaine is a victim of his own conscience and social pressure. Although *Moll* is a realistic picture of many parish housekeepers, it is essentially a very funny play. *The Chastitute*, in contrast, is a bitter satire; it portrays a man, conditioned by religion and custom, who has no alternative but to condemn himself to the slow suicide of drink.

Every parish had a Moll, by whatever name. Both her absolute devotion to the pastor and her control over the curates would be recognized quite easily by rural and urban audiences alike. John B. Keane remarked that "the people here know that until recent times Moll was the buffer between God and the common people. Moll was in many ways the voice of God, and there are many Molls."[3] Eileen Moriarty adds that, although Moll leads the curates to frustration by her tyranny, she is also a victim of Irish society; "by its attitude towards her, Irish society places the priest's housekeeper on the defensive and makes her into a supersensitive personality—thereby molding her into the very kind of person it criticizes her for being."[4] Keane says that he has known many housekeepers like Moll, most of whom worked hard in the parish but who kept the public at a distance from the Parish Priest. The play makes it clear that in the past of Keane's memory, it was acceptable for the pastor to be pampered, and the curates to be kept from mischief by hard work and a rigid diet. It is also clear that Moll's zeal for the parish often included a bonus for herself. While her motives are not always as clear to the pastor as they are to the audience, he seems content to keep the peace and to pass the responsibility for unpopular decisions to her. Keane recalls that the result of the housekeeper's prominence in parish life was more often bad than good because

> ... it meant that the Parish Priest rarely got in touch with his people—that he never came to the door, and to get in touch with people you must come to the door. ... If you send somebody to the door of your house all the time, people are going to stop coming.[5]

Like many spinsters, Moll derives her identity from her work. Her position, then, is a substitute for land and family, and her association with the Church gives her status in the local community. The identity of the housekeeper with her special role is such that any objection to her behavior is tantamount to criticism of the Parish Priest and the Church itself. In Keane's play, both the clerical stereotypes and the character of Moll are true enough to be recognized by almost any audience. In addition, Keane's exposé is a gentle prodding, and the result is a hearty laugh. It is so true to human nature that the most militant of the curates assumes the same stance as the Monsignor once he has been named Parish Priest. The pattern continues.

Keane concedes that the clergy-types that he depicts in *Moll* and *The Chastitute* belong to the era before the Second Vatican Council. He finds that younger priests today seem to have greater concern for ordinary parishioners than for administration. The author admits that he has been a severe critic of the Church. His remarks are directed toward the impersonal aspects of the institution and toward extremes in moral practice rather than toward theological or moral tenets. He finds great hope for the future in the Catholic Church in Ireland today. At the same time, Keane wonders whether there is still some failure of communication when people, in their search for direction, have abandoned the natural leadership of the Church and turned to supernatural manifestations. At the time of this interview, there was a great stir in Kerry and Cork because of statues that supposedly moved; many people gathered to pray at the sites, although there was no objective evidence of Divine intervention. While Keane finds the reports of these phenomena ridiculous, he nevertheless asserts that people are coming together to pray, and this in itself points to their needing something which is not being supplied by the institutional Church.[6]

The Chastitute presents two views of the clergy: the missioners who are part of John Bosco McLaine's memory and the Parish Priest who advises him in the present. The flashbacks recall the awe-inspiring figures of the visiting priests who would preach the parish mission, a period of renewal. The older style of preaching, which Keane portrays here, was guaranteed to inspire all listeners with the fear of Hell, and the sixth commandment, with its code of behavior between the sexes, was always a major theme. Irish puritanism stems from the period when Irish men, forbidden to study for the priesthood at home, were educated in France. There they were exposed to the tenets of Jansenism. This counterreform movement was conservative and unorthodox and was condemned by the Church in the seventeenth century. The movement had both theological and political facets, of which moral rigorism is only one part. The moral austerity, however, had a particular appeal for the Irish clergy, and extreme conservatism continued to mark the Irish Church long after the movement itself had died.

John Bosco McLaine's memory of the missioners and their tirades against close dancing and evil thoughts makes them grotesque figures that haunt his consciousness (C 9–10). Keane's exaggeration serves to point up the extremes of conservatism, while his understanding portrayal of John Bosco's confessor provides another view against which the extremes can be evaluated. McLaine, unfortunately, cannot benefit from the priest's advice and his assurance that normal sexual urgings do not constitute sin. McLaine is, in Keane's word, a chastitute:

> . . . a person without orders who has never lain down with a woman. He or she, as the case may be, is a rustic celibate by force of circumstance, peculiar to country-sides where the Catholic tradition of lifelong sexual abstemiousness is encouraged by the Catholic Church under whose strictures free-range sex is absolutely taboo. (C 25)

Keane treats sex openly and with sympathy. Even in his early plays, such as *Sharon's Grave*, he deals with the frustrations of unhealthy sexuality and every individual's need for love. Thomas Duff records Keane's response to an inquiry about his use of sex as a symbol for the human condition. The playwright notes the "dreadful attitude toward sex in Ireland. . . . Men and women concealed the fact that a physical longing existed. It was seen as something to be ashamed of."[7] This view opens up the traditional Irish motifs of land, religion, and politics to admit other impulses of human nature to the stage. Thus, sexual themes and the struggle for identity and influence demand equal attention with the older themes as indicators of a sense of place.

In *The Chastitute*, as in his other plays, Keane speaks his mind through the humor generated by the grotesque characters and a character who serves as spokesman. The exaggerated poses of the missioners would stimulate both recognition and a smile in an Irish audience. The chastitute himself is both comic in his bungling relationships and almost tragic in his frustrations. Underneath these characterizations the voice of Father Kimmerley calls for understanding and compassion for all the chastitutes of rural Ireland. Here, as in *Moll* and *The Crazy Wall*, Keane draws on the cultural conditions of the small towns. He peoples his plays with distinctive characters who create a place which is undeniably Irish. His particular gift of recreating the larger-than-life figures of the Kerry countryside permits his love of place to form a foundation for his social criticism.

Notes

Introduction

1. Robert Hogan, *Seven Irish Plays* (Minneapolis: University Press of Minnesota, 1967), 3.
2. Hogan, *Seven*, 28.
3. Gus Smith, interview with author, Dublin, Ireland, 3 July 1991.
4. Brian Cleeve, "The Short Story Teller" in *Fifty Years Young*, ed. John M. Feehan (Cork: The Mercier Press, 1979), 35.

Chapter 1. Landscape of a Writer

1. Sean O'Faolain, *The Irish: A Character Study* (New York: The Devin-Adair Company, 1949), 35.
2. John B. Keane, interview with author, Listowel, Co. Kerry, Ireland, 11 October 1985.
3. Susan and Thomas Cahill, *A Literary Guide to Ireland* (New York: Charles Scribner's Sons, 1973), 65.
4. Gus Smith, interview, 3 July 1991.
5. Ibid.
6. James N. Healy, interview with author, Cork, Ireland, 15 October 1985.
7. Eileen Moriarty, "John B. Keane: Kerry Dramatist" (Ph.D. diss., University of Washington, 1980), 206.
8. John B. Keane, interview with author, Listowel, Co. Kerry, Ireland, 18 June 1991.
9. Ben Barnes, interview with author, Dublin, Ireland, 5 July 1991.
10. Ibid.
11. Ibid.
12. Gus Smith, interview, 3 July 1991.
13. Mary Keane, interview with author, Listowel, Co. Kerry, Ireland, 19 June 1991.
14. John B. Keane, interview, 18 June 1991.

Chapter 2. Sense of Place, National Identity, and Irish Drama

1. E. Estyn Evans, *The Personality of Ireland: Habitat, Heritage and History* (Cambridge: Cambridge University Press, 1973), 66.
2. O'Faolain, *The Irish: A Character Study*, 3–4.
3. Evans, *Personality*, 66.

4. William Dumbleton, *Ireland: Life and Land in Literature* (Albany: State University of New York Press, 1984), 87.

5. Ibid.

6. Ann Saddlemyer, "The Cult of the Celt: Pan-Celticism in the Nineties" in *The World of W. B. Yeats*, rev. ed., ed. Robin Skelton and Ann Saddlemyer (Seattle: University Press of Washington, 1967), 3.

7. See Ulf Dantanus, *Brian Friel: The Growth of an Irish Dramatist*, Gothenburg Studies in English (Goteburg, Sweden: Acta Universitatis Gothoburgensis, 1985).

8. August Strindberg, "Miss Julie" in *Eight Best Plays*, trans. Edwin Bjorkman and N. Ericksen (1949; reprint, London: Duckworth, 1979), 117.

9. Ibid., 156.

10. John Louis Styan, *Drama, Stage and Audience* (London: Cambridge University Press, 1975), 35.

11. D.E.S. Maxwell, *A Critical History of Modern Irish Drama 1891–1980* (Cambridge: Cambridge University Press, 1984), 35.

12. Ernest Boyd, *The Contemporary Drama of Ireland* (Dublin: Talbot, 1918), 5.

13. Andrew E. Malone, *The Irish Drama* (London: Constable, 1929), 77.

14. Brenda Katz Clarke, *The Emergence of the Irish Peasant Play at the Abbey Theatre* (Ann Arbor, Mich.: University Microfilms International Research, 1982), 94.

15. Hazard Adams, *Lady Gregory* (Lewisburg, Pa.: Bucknell University Press, 1973), 29.

16. Isabella Augusta Gregory, *Our Irish Theatre* (New York: G. P. Putnam's Sons, 1913), 96.

17. George J. Watson, *Irish Identity and the Literary Revival* (New York: Barnes and Noble Books, 1979), 70.

18. Ernest A. Boyd, *Ireland's Literary Renaissance*, 3d ed. (New York: Barnes and Noble Books, 1968), 339.

19. Austin Clarke, "Introduction" in *Dramatic Fantasies*, vol. 1 of *The Plays of George Fitzmaurice* (Dublin: Dolmen Press, 1967), viii.

20. Catherine Middleton, "Roots and Rootlessness: An Exploration of the Concept in the Life and Novels of George Eliot" in *Humanistic Geography and Literature*, ed. Douglas C. D. Pocock (Totowa, N.J.: Barnes and Noble Books, 1981), 102.

Chapter 3. Dramatic Devices and the Sense of Place

1. Robert Hogan, *After the Irish Renaissance: A Critical History of Irish Drama since "The Plough and the Stars"* (Minneapolis: University Press of Minnesota, 1967), 208.

2. John B. Keane, "A Last Instalment," in *The World of Brendan Behan*, ed. Sean McCann (New York: Twayne Publishers, 1965), 202.

3. "Talking to John B. Keane," *Walkways*, prod. Pat Leahy (Dublin: RTE Radio, 23 September 1985).

4. W. G. Fay and Catherine Carswell, *The Fays of the Abbey Theatre* (London: Rich & Cowan Ltd., 1935), 200.

5. Conrad M. Arensberg, *The Irish Countryman* (1937; reprint, Garden City, N.Y.: The Natural History Press, 1968), 38–39.

6. Ibid., 55.

7. Hogan, *After Irish Renaissance*, 212.

8. John Millington Synge, *In Wicklow and West Kerry* (Dublin: Maunsel & Co. Ltd., 1912), 3.

9. Fintan O'Toole, "Sive—The Ritual Dimension," program notes, *Sive* by John B. Keane, dir. Ben Barnes (Dublin: Abbey Theatre, 1985).

10. Clarke, *Irish Peasant Play*, 132.

11. Ibid.

12. Maureen Waters, *The Comic Irishman* (Albany: State University of New York Press, 1984), 67.

13. Ibid., 68.

14. Synge, *Wicklow*, 1.

15. Paul F. Bothroyd, "The Years of the Travellers: Tinkers, Tramps and Travellers in Early Twentieth-Century Irish Drama and Society" in *Anglo-Irish Literature*, ed. Heinz Kosak (Bonn: Bouvier, 1982), 168.

Chapter 4. Stage Use of Language, Music, and Folk Customs

1. John B. Keane, interview with author, Listowel, Co. Kerry, Ireland, 11 October 1985.

2. Ibid.

3. Ibid.

4. Arthur McGuiness, *George Fitzmaurice* (Lewisburg: Bucknell University Press, 1975), 14.

5. Jean-Michel Pannecoucke, "John Brendan Keane and the New Irish Rural Drama," in *Aspects of the Irish Theatre*, ed. Patrick Rafroidi, et al. (Paris: Editions universitaires, 1972), 141.

6. Hogan, *After Irish Renaissance*, 213.

7. William J. Smyth, "Explorations of Place," in *Ireland: Towards a Sense of Place*, ed. Joseph Lee (Cork: Cork University Press, 1985), 5.

8. Sean O'Suilleabhain, *Irish Wake Amusements* (Cork: The Mercier Press, 1967), 170.

9. Ibid., 173.

10. Estyn E. Evans, *Irish Folk Ways* (New York: Devin-Adair Inc., 1957), 292.

11. O'Suilleabhain, *Wake*, 165.

12. J. Anthony Gaughan, *Listowel and Its Vicinity* (Cork: The Mercier Press, 1973), 135.

13. John Millington Synge, *The Complete Plays*, introduction and notes by T. R. Henn (London: Eyre Methuen, 1981), 82.

14. *The Dolmen Boucicault*, ed. David Krause (Chester Springs: Dufour Editions, Inc., 1965), 226–27.

15. John B. Keane, interview, 11 October 1985.

16. Barry Cassin, interview with author, Dublin, Ireland. 9 October 1985; James N. Healy, interview with author, Cork, Ireland, 15 October 1885.

Chapter 5. Contexts for Social Criticism

1. Hogan, *Seven*, 26.

2. Arensburg, *Irish Countryman*, 81.

3. Ibid., 89.

4. Ibid., 91.

5.´ Ibid., 39.

6. Ibid., 46.

7. Phyllis Ryan, "John B's Women," in *Fifty Years Young*, ed. John M. Feehan (Cork: The Mercier Press, 1979), 63.

8. Moriarty, *Kerry Dramatist*, 150.

9. Ibid., 152.

Chapter 6. Lust for Land: *The Field* and *Big Maggie*

1. John B. Keane, interview, 11 October 1985.

2. Moriarty, *Kerry Dramatist*, 197.

3. Barry Cassin, interview, 9 October 1985.

4. Christopher Murray, interview with author, Dublin, Ireland, 5 November 1985.

5. Barry Cassin, interview, 9 October 1985.

6. Ben Barnes, interview, 5 July 1991.

7. Christopher Murray, interview with author, Rathdrum, Co. Wicklow, Ireland, 25 June 1991.

8. Gus Smith, interview, 3 July 1991.

9. Ben Barnes, interview, 5 July 1991.

10. John B. Keane, interview, 18 June 1991.

11. Barry Cassin, interview, 9 October 1985.

12. John B. Keane, interview, 11 October 1985.

Chapter 7. Separation from the Land

1. Gabriel Fallon, "Dublin's Fourth Theatre Festival," *Modern Drama* 5 (1962): 23.

2. Hans-Georg Stalder, *Anglo-Irish Peasant Drama: The Motifs of Land and Emigration* (Bern: Pater Lang, 1978), 67.

3. John B. Keane, interview, 11 October 1985.

4. Moriarty, *Kerry Dramatist*, 159.

5. John B. Keane, interview, 11 October 1985.

6. Ibid.

7. Thomas A. Duff, "Ireland's Lusty Scourge—John B. Keane," in *Fifty Years Young*, ed. John M. Feehan (Cork: The Mercier Press, 1979), 23.

Bibliography

Adams, Hazard. *Lady Gregory.* Lewisburg, Pa.: Bucknell University Press, 1973.

Arensberg, Conrad M. *The Irish Countryman.* 1937. Reprint. Garden City, N.Y.: The Natural History Press, 1968.

Barnes, Ben. Interview with author. Dublin, Ireland, 5 July 1991.

Barnes, Bettina. "Irish Travelling People." In *Gypsies, Tinkers and Other Travellers,* edited by Farnaham Rehfisch, 231–56. London: Academic Press, 1975.

Barrett, John. "Some Trends in Contemporary Irish Drama." *Prompts* 1(1981): 8–10.

Beckerman, Bernard. *Dynamics of Drama: Theory and Method of Analysis.* New York: Alfred A. Knopf, Inc., 1970.

Botheroyd, Paul F. "The Years of the Travellers: Tinkers, Tramps and Travellers in Early Twentieth-Century Irish Drama and Society." In *Anglo-Irish Literature,* edited by Heinz Kosak, 167–75. Bonn: Bouvier, 1982.

Boucicault, Dion. *The Dolmen Boucicault.* Edited by David Krause. Chester Springs, Pa.: Dufour Editions, Inc., 1965.

Boyd, Ernest A. *The Contemporary Drama of Ireland.* Dublin: Talbot, 1918.

———. *Ireland's Literary Renaissance.* 3d ed. New York: Barnes and Noble Books, 1968.

Brown, Malcolm. *The Politics of Irish Literature.* Seattle: University Press of Washington, 1972.

Brown, Terence. *Ireland: A Social and Cultural History 1922–1979.* London: Collins Books, 1981.

Cahill, Susan, and Thomas Cahill. *A Literary Guide to Ireland.* New York: Charles Scribner's Sons, 1973.

Carpenter, Andrew, ed. *Place, Personality and the Irish Writer.* Irish Literary Studies I. New York: Barnes and Noble Books, 1977.

Cassin, Barry. Interview with author. Dublin, Ireland, 9 October 1985.

———. "Introduction." In *The Highest House on the Mountain* by John B. Keane. Dublin: Progress House, 1961.

Clarke, Austin. "Introduction." In *The Plays of George Fitzmaurice.* Vol. 1, *Dramatic Fantasies.* Dublin: The Dolmen Press, 1967.

Clarke, Brenna Katz. *The Emergence of the Irish Peasant Play at the Abbey Theatre.* Ann Arbor, Mich.: University Microfilms International Research, 1982.

Cleeve, Brian. "The Short Story Teller." In *Fifty Years Young,* edited by John M. Feehan, 31–40. Cork: The Mercier Press, 1979.

Colum, Padraic. *Three Plays.* Rev. ed. New York: Macmillan Co., 1925.

Comiskey, Ray. "A Hundred Key People in Irish Theatre." *The Irish Times,* 20 June 1985, 12.

Connolly, Peter, ed. *Literature and the Changing Ireland.* Gerards Cross: Colin Smythe Ltd., 1982.

Corkery, Daniel. *Synge and Anglo-Irish Literature.* London: Longmans, 1931.

Dantanus, Ulf. *Brian Friel: The Growth of an Irish Dramatist.* Gothenburg Studies in English. Goteburg, Sweden: Acta Universitatis Gothoburgensis, 1985.

———. "Time for a New Irish Playwright?" *Moderna Sprak* 71 (1977): 37–47.

"Discussion on Irish Theatre Misfired." *The Irish Times,* 27 February 1961, 5.

Donoghue, Denis. "The Problems of Being Irish." *Times Literary Supplement,* 17 March 1972, 291–92.

Donovan, Dan. "Foreword." In *The Man from Clare* by John B. Keane, 9–10. Cork: The Mercier Press, 1962.

Duff, Thomas A. "Ireland's Lusty Scourge: John B. Keane." In *Fifty Years Young,* edited by John M. Feehan, 19–29. Cork: The Mercier Press, 1979.

Duggan, George Chester. *The Stage Irishman.* London: Longmans, 1937.

Dumbleton, William A. *Ireland: Life and Land in Literature.* Albany: State University of New York Press, 1984.

Durrell, Lawrence. *Spirit of Place.* Edited by Alan G. Thomas. New York: E. P. Dutton Inc., 1969.

Evans, E. Estyn. *Irish Folk Ways.* New York: Devin-Adair, Inc., 1957.

———. *The Personality of Ireland: Habitat, Heritage and History.* London: Cambridge University Press, 1973.

Fallis, Richard. *The Irish Renaissance.* Syracuse, N.Y.: Syracuse University Press, 1977.

Fallon, Gabriel. "Dublin's Fourth Theatre Festival." *Modern Drama* 5 (1962): 21–26.

Fay, W. G., and Catherine Carswell. *The Fays of the Abbey Theatre.* London: Rich & Cowan Ltd., 1935.

Feehan, John M., ed. *Fifty Years Young: A Tribute to John B. Keane.* Cork: The Mercier Press, 1979.

Fitzmaurice, George. *The Plays of George Fitzmaurice.* 3 vols. Dublin: The Dolmen Press, 1957.

Foster, John Wilson. "The Geography of Irish Fiction." In *The Irish Novel in Our Time,* edited by Patrick Rafroidi and Maurice Harmon, 89–103. Villeneuve-d'Ascq: Universite de Lille, 1975–76.

Fox, R. M. "Social Criticism in the Irish Theatre." *Aryan Path* 38 (1967): 179–81.

Gaughan, J. Anthony. *Listowel and Its Vicinity.* Cork: The Mercier Press, 1973.

Gillespie, Elgie. "The Saturday Interview: John B. Keane." *The Irish Times,* 19 June 1976, 5.

Gmelch, Sharon. *Tinkers and Travellers.* Montreal: McGill University Press, 1975.

Graves, R. B. "The Stage Irishman Among the Irish." *Theatre History Studies* 1 (1981): 29–38.

Gregory, Isabella Augusta. *Our Irish Theatre.* New York: G. P. Putnam's Sons, 1913.

———. *Selected Plays.* Chosen and introduced by Elizabeth Coxhead. London: G. P. Putnam's Sons, 1952.

————. *Visions and Beliefs in the West of Ireland.* New York: G. P. Putnam's Sons, 1920.

Harmon, Maurice. "Literature and Nationalism in Ireland since 1922." *Kwartolnik Neofilologiczny* 25 (1978): 473–86.

Healy, James N. "The Birth of *Sive*." In *Fifty Years Young,* edited by John M. Feehan, 9–17. Cork: The Mercier Press, 1979.

————. "Foreword." In *Sharon's Grave,* by John B. Keane, vi–vii. Dublin: Progress House, 1960.

————. Interview with author. Cork, Ireland, 15 October 1985.

Hogan, Robert. *After the Irish Renaissance: A Critical History of Irish Drama since "The Plough and the Stars."* Minneapolis: University Press of Minnesota, 1967.

————. *Seven Irish Plays.* Minneapolis: University Press of Minnesota, 1967.

————. "The Art and Craft of John B. Keane." In *Fifty Years Young,* edited by John M. Feehan, 79–89. Cork: The Mercier Press, 1979.

————. *"Since O'Casey" and Other Essays on Irish Drama.* Totowa, N.J.: Barnes and Noble Books, 1983.

————. "Where Have All the Shamrocks Gone?" In *Aspects of the Irish Theatre,* edited by Patrick Rafroidi, Raymonde Popot, and William Parker, 261–71. Paris: Editions universitaires, 1972.

Hunt, Hugh. *The Abbey: Ireland's National Theatre 1904–1979.* New York: Columbia University Press, 1979.

Ibsen, Henrik. *Eleven Plays.* Introduction by H. L. Mencken. New York: Random House, n.d.

"John B. Keane's Listowel." *My Own Place.* Prod. John Williams. RTE TV, Dublin. 7 May 1980.

Keane, John B. "A Last Instalment." *The World of Brendan Behan.* Edited by Sean McCann. New York: Twayne Publishers, Inc., 1965. 201–5.

————. *The Year of the Hiker.* Prod. Tim Danaher. RTE Radio, Dublin. 25 October 1975.

————. Interview with author. Listowel, Co. Kerry, Ireland, 11 October 1985.

————. Interview with author. Listowel, Co. Kerry, Ireland, 18 June 1991.

Keane, Mary. Interview with author. Listowel, Co. Kerry, Ireland, 19 June 1991.

Kosok, Heinz, ed. *Studies in Anglo-Irish Literature.* Bonn: Bouvier, 1982.

Krause, David. "The Theatre of Dion Boucicault." In *The Dolmen Boucicault,* 9–47. Chester Springs, Pa.: Dufour Editions, Inc., 1965.

————. *The Profane Book of Irish Comedy.* Ithaca, N.Y.: Cornell University Press, 1982.

Lee, Joseph, ed. *Ireland: Towards a Sense of Place.* Cork: Cork University Press, 1985.

Linehan, Fergus, Hugh Leonard, John B. Keane, and Brian Friel. "The Future of Irish Drama." *The Irish Times,* 12 February 1970, 14.

Lutwack, Leonard. *The Role of Place in Literature.* Syracuse, N.Y.: Syracuse University Press, 1984.

McCartney, Donal. "The Quest for Irish Political Identity: The Image and the Illusion." In *Image and Illusion: Anglo-Irish Literature and Its Contexts,* edited by Maurice Harmon. 13–22. Dublin: Wolfhound Press, 1979.

McGuinness, Arthur. *George Fitzmaurice*. The Irish Writers Series. Lewisburg, Pa.: Bucknell University Press, 1975.

Malone, Andrew E. *The Irish Drama*. London: Constable, 1929.

Maxwell, D.E.S. *A Critical History of Modern Irish Drama 1891–1980*. Cambridge: Cambridge University Press, 1984.

Mercier, Vivian. *The Irish Comic Tradition*. Oxford: Clarendon Press, 1952.

Middleton, Catherine A. "Roots and Rootlessness: An Exploration of the Concept in the Life and Novels of George Eliot." In *Humanistic Geography and Literature*, edited by Douglas C. D. Pocock, 101–20. Totowa, N.J.: Barnes and Noble Books, 1981.

Moriarty, Eileen Marie. "John B. Keane: Kerry Dramatist." Ph.D. diss., University of Washington, 1980.

Moseley, Virginia. "A Week in Dublin." *Modern Drama* 4 (1961): 164–71.

Murray, Christopher. "Irish Drama in Transition 1966–1978." *Etudes Irlandaises* 4 Nouvelle serie (1979): 287–308.

———. "Recent Irish Drama." In *Studies in Anglo-Irish Literature*, edited by Heinz Kosok, 439–46. Bonn: Bouvier, 1982.

———. Interviews with author. Dublin, Ireland, 2 October 1985 and 5 November 1985.

———. Interview with author. Rathdrum, Co. Wicklow, Ireland, 25 June 1991.

O'Driscoll, Robert, ed. *Theatre and Nationalism in Twentieth-Century Ireland*. Toronto: University of Toronto Press, 1971.

O'Faolain, Sean. *The Irish: A Character Study*. New York: The Devin-Adair Company, 1949.

O'hAodha, Micheal. "Foreword." In *Sive*, by John B. Keane, 5–6. Dublin Progress House, 1959.

———. Letter to author, 24 December 1985.

———. "Sive—a Portent!" Program notes. *Sive* By John B. Keane. Dir. Ben Barnes. Abbey Theatre, Dublin, 1985.

———. Telephone conversation with author, 11 November 1985.

Orel, Harold. "Synge's Concept of the Tramp." *Eire-Ireland* 7 (1972): 55–61.

O'Suilleabhain, Sean. *Irish Wake Amusements*. Cork: The Mercier Press, 1967.

O'Toole, Fintan. "Today: Contemporary Theatre—The Illusion of Tradition." In *Ireland and the Arts*, edited by Tim Pat Coogan, 132–37. London: Namara, 1983.

———. "Sive—The Ritual Dimension." Program notes. *Sive*. By John B. Keane. Dir. Ben Barnes. Abbey Theatre, Dublin, 1985.

———. "Introduction." In *Three Plays: Sive, The Field, Big Maggie*, by John B. Keane, edited by Ben Barnes, 7–8. Cork: The Mercier Press, 1990.

O'Tuama, Sean. "Stability and Ambivalence: Aspects of the Sense of Place and Religion in Irish Literature." In *Ireland: Towards a Sense of Place*, edited by Joseph Lee, 21–33. Cork: Cork University Press, 1985.

Pannecoucke, Jean-Michel. "John Brendan Keane and the New Irish Rural Drama." In *Aspects of the Irish Theatre*, edited by Patrick Rafroidi, Raymonde Popot and William Parker, 137–45. Paris: Editions universitaires, 1972.

Parkin, Andrew. "Imagination's Abode: The Symbolism of House Settings in

Modern Irish Stage Plays." In *Myth and Reality in Irish Literature*, edited by Joseph Ronsley, 255–63. Waterloo, Ont.: Wilfred Laurier University Press, 1977.

Pocock, Douglas, C. D. *Humanistic Geography and Literature: Essays on the Experience of Place*. Totowa, N.J.: Barnes and Noble Books, 1981.

Porter, Raymond J. "The Irish Messianic Tradition." *The Emory University Quarterly* XXII (1966): 29–35.

Rafroidi, Patrick, Raymonde, and William Parker, eds. *Aspects of the Irish Theatre*. Paris: Editions universitaires, 1972.

———. "From Listowel with Love: John B. Keane and Bryan MacMahon." In *The Irish Short Story*, edited by Patrick Rafroidi and Terence Brown, 263–73. Gerrards Cross: Colin Smythe Ltd., 1979.

Rehfisch, Farnham, ed. *Gypsies, Tinkers and Other Travellers*. London: Academic Press, 1975.

Reynolds, Lorna. "Irish Women in Legend, Literature and Life." In *Women in Irish Legend, Life and Literature*, edited by S. F. Gallagher, 11–25. Gerrards Cross: Colin Smythe Ltd., 1983.

Ronsley, Joseph, ed. *Myth and Reality in Irish Literature*. Waterloo, Ont.: Wilfred Laurier University Press, 1977.

Rushe, Desmond. "Keane to Begin." *Eire-Ireland* 15 (1980):112–15.

Ryan, Phyllis. "John B.'s Women." In *Fifty Years Young*, edited by John M. Feehan, 61–72. Cork: The Mercier Press, 1979.

Saddlemyer, Ann. "The Cult of the Celt: Pan-Celticism in the Nineties." In *The World of W. B. Yeats*. Rev. ed., edited by Robin Skelton and Ann Saddlemyer, 3–5. Seattle: University Press of Washington, 1967.

Smith, Gus. *Festival Glory in Athlone*. Dublin: Aherlow Press, 1977.

———. Interview with author. Dublin, Ireland, 3 July 1991.

Smyth, William J. "Exploration of Place." In *Ireland: Towards a Sense of Place*, edited by Joseph Lee, 1–20. Cork: Cork University Press, 1985.

Stalder, Hans-Georg. *Anglo-Irish Peasant Drama: The Motifs of Land and Emigration*. Bern: Peter Lang, 1978.

Strindberg, August. "Miss Julie." In *Eight Best Plays*, translated by Edwin Bjorkman and N. Erichsen, 117–58. 1949. Reprint. London: Duckworth, 1979.

Styan, John Louis. *Drama, Stage and Audience*. London: Cambridge University Press, 1975.

Synge, John Millington. *In Wicklow and West Kerry*. Dublin: Maunsel and Co., Ltd., 1912.

———. *The Complete Plays*. Introduction and notes by T. R. Henn. The Master Playwrights Series. London: Eyre Methuen, 1981.

"Talking to John B. Keane." *Walkways*. Prod. Pat Leahy. RTE Radio, Dublin. 23 September 1985.

Walsh, Richard B. "Aspects of Irishness." In *Literature and Folk Culture: Ireland and Newfoundland*, edited by Alison Feder and Bernice Schrank, 7–31. St. John's, Newfoundland: Memorial University Press, 1977.

Waters, Maureen. *The Comic Irishman*. Albany: State University of New York Press, 1984.

Watson, George J. *Irish Identity and the Literary Revival.* New York: Barnes and Noble Books, 1979.

Winkler, Elizabeth Hale. "'Eejitin' About': Adolescence in Friel and Keane." *Eire-Ireland* 16 (1981): 138–44.

Yeats, William Butler. *The Collected Plays of W. B. Yeats.* New York: Macmillan Co., 1953.

Index

Regional identity, 18, 23. *See also* Land

Regional justice, 98–100. *See also* Informer; Law

Religion: as theme, 82, 89–91

Revivals, 16, 26–27

"Rising of the Moon, The," 41

Self-Portrait, 20, 112, 114

Sense of place, 30–31; basis of social criticism, 124; and national character, 46; and peasant plays, 37. *See also* Place

Setting: cottage, 50–51, 53; double vista, 51–53; social constraints, 52–53; symbol, 55; terrain, 53–55

Sexuality, 83, 91–92, 108–9; repression of, 111, 122–24. *See also* Isolation

Sexual mores: as theme, 22

Sharon's Grave, 22, 69–70, 91, 112; setting, 51–52; wanderer, 63; wake, 77–81

Sive, 14, 16, 21–22, 26, 122; and Abbey Theatre, 21; language, 70, 72; regional characters, 57–61; strong women, 84–87

Smith, Gus, 14, 27, 108

Social comment, 82–83, 110

Social conventions, 105–9, 116

Songs, 60, 64, 70–74

Southern Theatre Group, 21

Spiritual exile, 23, 120. *See also* Isolation

Sports, 22–23, 117

"Spreading the News," 40–42

Stage Irishman, 37, 63, 93, 95

Stereotypes: of Irish nationality, 29, 83–84; of Irish women, 103–4

Stranger, 51–52, 65, 94. *See also* Outsider; Wanderer

Strindberg, August, 33–35

Superstition, 65–66

Synge, John Millington, 39, 42–45, 63, 67, 75–77

Terrain: bog, 54–55

Themes, 22–23, 82–83, 89–91, 111

Tomelty, Joseph, 20

Traditional themes, 82

Traveling men, 72–73. *See also* Outsider; Wanderer

Urban setting, 24

Violence, 83, 93–102

Wake, 74–81. *See also* Regional characters

Wanderer, 62–64. *See also* Outsider; Stranger

Women, 84–87, 92, 103–4, 109–10

Year of the Hiker, The, 22, 26, 52–53, 86–90; authority in the family, 87–89, 118; wanderer, 63–65